Warrior • 117

French Resistance Fighter

France's Secret Army

Terry Crowdy · Illustrated by Steve Noon

First published in Great Britain in 2007 by Osprey Publishing,
PO Box 883, Oxford, OX1 9PL, UK
PO Box 3985, New York, NY 10185-3985, USA
Email: info@ospreypublishing.com

Osprey Publishing is part of the Osprey Group.

Transferred to digital print on demand 2014

First published 2007
3rd impression 2009

Printed and bound by Cadmus Communications, USA.

A CIP catalogue record for this book is available from the British Library

ISBN: 978 1 84603 076 5

Page layout by Mark Holt
Index by Peter Rea
Originated by PDQ Digital Media Solutions, UK
Typeset in Helvetica Neue and ITC New Baskerville

Artist's note

Readers may care to note that the original paintings from which the colour plates in this
book were prepared are available for private sale. All reproduction copyright whatsoever
is retained by the Publishers. All enquiries should be addressed to:

www.steve-noon.co.uk

The Publishers regret that they can enter into no correspondence upon this matter.

Acknowledgements

I would like to thank the staff at the British Library and the Imperial War Museum
Photograph Archive for their kind assistance. Thanks also to Yves Martin, the very
talented Simon Robinson and last but not least my wife, Sarah.

The Woodland Trust

Osprey Publishing is supporting the Woodland Trust, the UK's leading woodland
conservation charity, by funding the dedication of trees.

www.ospreypublishing.com

Abbreviations

AS	Armée Secrète	FFI	Forces Françaises de l'Intérieur
BCRA	Bureau Central de Renseignements et d'Action	FN	Front National
CCZN	Comité de Coordination de Zone Nord	FTPF/FTP	Francs-Tireurs et Partisans Français
CDLL	Ceux de la Libération	MOI	Main d'Oeuvre Immigrée
CDLR	Ceux de la Résistance	MUR	Mouvements Unis de Résistance
CE	commissaire aux effectifs	OCM	Organisation Civile et Militaire
CFLN	Comité Français de la Libération Nationale	OG	Operational Group
CMN	Comité Militaire National	ORA	Organisation de Résistance de l'Armée
CMR	Comité Militaire Régional	OS	Organisation Spéciale
CMRI	Comité Militaire Inter-Régional	OSS	Office of Strategic Services
CMZ	Comité Militaire de Zone Sud	PCF	Parti Communiste Français
CND	Confrérie de Notre Dame	ROP	Recrutement, Organisation, Propagande
CNR	Couseil National de la Résistance	SFHQ	Special Force Headquarters
CO	commissaire aux operations	SHAEF	Supreme Headquarters Allied Expeditionary Force
COMAC	Comité Militaire d'Action	SOE	Special Operations Executive
CT	commissaire technique	STO	Service du Travail Obligatoire
EMFFI	État Major des Forces Françaises de l'Intérieur	UNE	Union Nacional Espanola

CONTENTS

FRENCH RESISTANCE FIGHTER: FRANCE'S SECRET ARMY

INTRODUCTION

On 10 May 1940 the Nazi Blitzkrieg was unleashed on Western Europe. By the end of the month, Holland and Belgium were overrun and a shattered British Army could do nothing but extricate itself from the beaches of Dunkirk. Two weeks into June and the Germans were in Paris. With millions of refugees on the road, 90,000 French soldiers dead and 1.8 million more in captivity, on 17 June France's Great War hero, Marshal Pétain, asked for an armistice.

Hitler humiliated France. Mirroring the fate of the German Army in 1918, the French 'Armistice Army' was limited to 100,000 men. France was partitioned. The disputed region of Alsace-Lorraine was placed under German civil administration, while the *départements* of Pas-de-Calais and Nord came under the authority of occupied Belgium. The remainder of France was split into two zones. The northern zone, which included the entire Channel and Atlantic coastline, was occupied by the Germans. The southern zone was self-governed by the French, albeit with heavy strings attached.

Unoccupied France was governed from the town of Vichy. Initially almost everyone rallied round the 84-year-old Pétain, who became head of state. The old marshal was identified with the heroic defence of Verdun in 1916 and people believed he would again see them through difficult times. They hoped Pétain was playing the Germans at a double game and was secretly planning the liberation of France. A very effective propaganda campaign blamed defeat on British self-interest. This idea was strongly reinforced when Britain attacked the French Navy at Mers-el-Kébir to prevent it falling into German hands – almost 1,300 French sailors were killed by the British. Few heard the BBC broadcast made by General Charles de Gaulle on 18 June 1940. Self-proclaimed chief of the 'Free French' in London, de Gaulle urged Frenchmen not to lose hope. His broadcast closed defiantly: 'whatever happens, the flame of French Resistance must not and will not be extinguished.' Many thought him a traitor. Pétain sentenced de Gaulle and his followers to death in their absence.

Freedom fighters to some, terrorists and gangsters to others; two dusty maquisards armed with American submachine guns. Allied Supreme Command (SHAEF) was not sure what to make of the Resistance before the D-Day landings, fearing it would melt away when the fighting started. However, its performance in cutting German transport and communication networks and sapping enemy reserves and morale led Allied commander Eisenhower to declare it worth 15 divisions of infantry. (IWM KY34412)

The shock of defeat. As German soldiers march into Paris on 14 June 1940, a Frenchman weeps among a crowd of shocked onlookers. Although the vast majority of the French wanted nothing more than to go about their daily routines, it became increasingly difficult not to choose between collaboration and resistance. (NARA 535896)

STO *réfractaires* in the summer of 1943. Although the Germans were at pains to present it as anything but, the STO was little other than slave labour. By deporting these young men to Germany, the Reich only succeeded in forcing people to join the Resistance when they otherwise might not have done. (IWM MH11169)

Vichy France became a repressive, anti-democratic society. Individuals were victimized because of left-wing beliefs and Freemasonry was prohibited. France played its part in the Holocaust too. Between March 1942 and July 1944, almost 76,000 Jews were deported from France to the death camps. In May 1942 the Nazis demanded 250,000 French workers for service in Germany. Known as *la relève* (the relief), this voluntary scheme failed and was replaced in February 1943 by the *Service du Travail Obligatoire* (Compulsory Work Service; STO) – the forced conscription of workers. More than 600,000 French civilians were deported to work in Nazi industry. If things were not bad enough, in response to Allied successes in the Mediterranean, the Nazis crossed the line of demarcation and occupied the southern zone in November 1942, sweeping away the last pretences of French sovereignty. The Vichy army was disarmed and replaced by a 30,000-strong secret police force known as the *Milice* (Militia). An ugly stain on French history, the *Milice* was led by Joseph Darnand, who took a personal oath of loyalty to Hitler and received the rank of Sturmbannführer in Himmler's SS.

Against this miserable backdrop, of which the above is merely a snapshot, acts of resistance began to emerge. Starved of news, clandestine newspapers and journals began to appear, reporting the stories that Nazi propagandists suppressed. From clandestine press to direct action, the urge to take up arms followed. As young men and women fled into the hills to avoid compulsory service in Germany, the ranks of the maquis

A maquis member in the Limousin region duplicating clandestine leaflets. The written word was a powerful tool of the Resistance in promoting free speech, news from the Allies and pointing out German crimes. Groups like the *Francs-Tireurs et Partisans Français* (FTP) also produced their own training manuals using printing presses and duplicators like the one shown here. (IWM MH11132)

swelled by the spring of 1944. Living as outlaws, poorly armed, mostly without uniforms and always terminally short of cigarettes, the men and women of the Resistance nevertheless played an effective part in their own liberation.

CHRONOLOGY

1939
1 September   German invasion of Poland
3 September   Britain and France declare war on Germany

1940
10 May   German offensive opens in the West
14 May   German Army breaks through French lines at Sedan
27 May   Capitulation of Belgian Army
28 May–3 `   Dunkirk evacuation
6 June   Germans break through French lines on the Somme
10 June   French government moves to Bordeaux
14 June   Paris occupied by the Germans
16 June   Marshal Pétain becomes Prime Minister
17 June   Pétain requests an armistice; General de Gaulle arrives in London
18 June   Appeal for Resistance by de Gaulle on the BBC
2 July   Pétain becomes head of state of new government at Vichy
3 July   English fleet attacks French Navy at Mers-el-Kébir
19 July   Formation of Special Operations Executive (SOE)
2 August   De Gaulle is sentenced to death by Pétain
11 November   Student protest on the Champs-Élysées

1941
15 May   Communist resistance movement *Front National* (National Front; NF) is created
22 June   Beginning of German offensive against USSR
21 August   First German officer assassinated by a French communist
8 October   Free French secret service agency the *Bureau Central de Renseignements et d'Action* (Central Office for Intelligence and Action; BCRA) is formed

20 October	Jean Moulin reaches London to lobby for support for the Resistance
1 November	Henri Frenay founds the *Combat* movement
7 December	Japan attacks Pearl Harbor
11 December	Germany declares war on United States

1942

2 January	Jean Moulin is parachuted into southern zone as de Gaulle's representative
27 March	First deportation of French Jews to Auschwitz
1 May	Patriotic demonstrations throughout the southern zone
29 May	French Jews forced to wear the yellow star in Occupied Zone
22 June	Vichy Prime Minister Pierre Laval introduces *la relève*. For every three workers sent to Germany, one prisoner of war is returned
14 July	Demonstrations in the southern zone mark 'Bastille Day'
19 August	Allied raid on Dieppe fails with heavy losses
11 November	Germans invade Unoccupied Zone and disarm the Armistice Army
27 November	Vichy fleet scuttles its ships in Toulon
1 December	General Frère founds the *Organisation de Résistance de l'Armée* (Army Resistance Organization; ORA)

1943

26 January	Creation of the *Mouvements Unis de Résistance* (United Resistance Movements; MUR)
30 January	Creation of the *Milice*
2 February	German Army at Stalingrad surrenders
16 February	Mobilization of men for the STO
12 May	Rommel's Afrika Korps capitulates in Tunisia
27 May	Foundation of *Conseil National de la Résistance* (National Council of the Resistance; CNR)
30 May	De Gaulle arrives in Algeria
3 June	The *Comité Français de la Libération Nationale* (French National Liberation Committee; CFLN) is formed
9 June	General Delestraint arrested in Paris and sent to Dachau
21 June	Jean Moulin arrested by Klaus Barbie
5 September	Corsica liberated

1944

1 February	Creation of the *Forces Françaises de l'Intérieur* (French Forces of the Interior; FFI)
23 March	General Koenig is appointed commander-in-chief of the FFI
20 April	German troops attack the Vercors maquis
5 June	The Resistance receives messages via the BBC announcing the forthcoming invasion
6 June	D-Day: Allies land in Normandy
10 June	Germans massacre 642 civilian victims at Oradour-sur-Glane
14 June	De Gaulle lands in Normandy
15 August	Operation *Anvil* – Allied landings in Provence
19 August	Beginning of Paris uprising
25 August	Liberation of Paris
26 August	De Gaulle on the Champs-Élysées
31 August	Provisional French government transfers from Algeria to Paris
3 September	Lyons is liberated
7 September	Pétain and Laval go to Germany
1 October	Allies reach German border
23 November	Liberation of Strasbourg

1945

26 April	Pétain returns to France
7 May	The war ends in Europe
23 July–14 August	Trial of Pétain. The marshal is sentenced to death, but then pardoned by de Gaulle

MOTIVATIONS FOR RESISTANCE

The French Resistance remains a controversial subject in France. For some the Resistance fighters were heroes; for many they were terrorists, gangsters and even traitors. It was made up of a number of different groups and included civilians and service people of both sexes from all political persuasions, professions and ages. No one particular group had a monopoly over it. It has been estimated that 2 per cent of the French population (about 400,000) were active resisters, with some authorities claiming a figure as high as 5 per cent. In addition, there were perhaps no fewer than 10 per cent (2 million) who were passive resisters, sympathetic enough to read underground newspapers and turn a blind eye here and there.

Examining the complex motivations behind Resistance membership, we should perhaps begin with something as basic as xenophobia. Many Frenchmen had a simple and intense dislike of their German neighbours. This hostility was partly historical and stemmed from previous conflicts, notably World War I (1914–18) and the Franco-Prussian War (1870–71). French Teutophobes labelled their Germanic neighbours as *Boche*, or *Schleuh*, after a notoriously fierce Moroccan Berber tribe. Roger Millar, a British Special Operations Executive (SOE) agent working with the Resistance, remembered how Germans were also referred to as *Fritz*, *Stolls* and *Schloks*. Other interesting expressions included *doryphores* – after a parasite that fed on potatoes – and after 1941 the expression *frisé* (curly) came into usage. There was the insult *tête carrée* (lit. square head), a term originating in the eastern region of Lorraine hinting at excessive order, a lack of individuality and an absence of civility.

Xenophobia was dramatically increased by the German occupation and was exacerbated by a feeling of impotence against the invader. For young Frenchmen the presence of confident, martially successful Germans in their midst was too much. They were rankled by the sight of local girls hanging shamelessly onto the arm of a *Schleuh*. They resented the cinemas and restaurants reserved for exclusive German use and the inflated purchasing power of German currency. Joining the Resistance was a means of restoring self-respect and national pride.

A great many French men and women had no option but to join the Resistance because they were directly persecuted by the Nazis and the Vichy regime – notably Freemasons and Jews. When the compulsory labour draft was introduced, a significant number of draftees went on the run rather than submit to working in Germany. These *réfractaires* headed for the forests and mountains and were said to have 'taken to the *maquis*' – a Corsican word

Interior of a maquis hut showing the sleeping arrangements. By many accounts such arrangements were by no means enjoyed by all maquis groups. (IWM MH11173)

referring to the inner terrain of hills and forests. Out of necessity, the *réfractaires* and others evading German persecution spontaneously banded together in small groups for mutual support, relying on local farmers and shepherds for aid. Faced with extra hungry mouths to feed, the farmers in turn went to local Resistance chiefs for assistance. It was not long before the Resistance realized the potential of those sheltering in the maquis and began recruiting them en masse and providing them with training.

Although perhaps not as prominent as the maquis, industrial groups such as *les Cheminots* (French railway workers) were also important, and because of the nature of their work found themselves in the forefront of both resistance and collaboration. Although only a minority of *Cheminots* were active members of the Resistance, their key positions meant they were among the most important and sought after. After the occupation in 1940, *Cheminots* gained a reputation for helping French and British soldiers to escape into unoccupied France, from where they could escape to Spain. They continued this by assisting the escape of Allied air crews, Jews and STO *réfractaires*. The *Cheminots* assisted with the distribution of clandestine newspapers through France, and passed important information to the Allied secret services about German transport movements. They also contributed to the preparation of *Plan Vert* – the plan to paralyse the French rail network during the period around D-Day.

Others resisted because Nazi doctrine was incompatible with their Christian faith. Countryside priests often helped Allied airmen and

Giraud, Roosevelt, de Gaulle and Churchill in Casablanca, January 1943. Resistance politics often overshadowed the work on the ground. Although they had their disagreements, at least Churchill had given de Gaulle a platform on which to build the Free French movement. Roosevelt detested de Gaulle and preferred General Giraud, who was also supported by the Vichy army resistance. (NARA 196990)

commandos evade capture out of a sense of compassion. In an area with a strong regional identity like Brittany, there was also a certain tradition of resistance to outside political control. For others political conviction was a motivation, and this secured the involvement of the left-wing movements – socialists, trade unionists and the like.

Perhaps surprisingly, communists only began to feature prominently in the Resistance after June 1941. One must remember how in 1939 the Soviet leader Josef Stalin had performed a political somersault and agreed a non-aggression pact with Hitler. This took communist supporters worldwide by surprise and caused many to resign from the party. When the Soviet Union went on to occupy part of Poland following the German invasion in September 1939 the *Parti Communiste Français* (French Communist Party; PCF) was banned in France. The organization went underground. At the end of September new instructions came out of Moscow via the Comintern (Communist International), instructing the PCF not to criticize Germany, but to denounce the conflict as an 'Imperialist War' undertaken by Britain and France.

Although officially toeing the Moscow line, French communists began resisting at a grass roots level, securing weapons and, in October 1940, forming an *Organisation Spéciale* (OS) that carried out a number of attacks, setting fire to stores bound for Germany and blocking roads. The cadres of the OS were often veterans of the International Brigade that had fought in the Spanish Civil War (1936–39) against the right-wing nationalist General Franco. When Hitler broke his treaty with Stalin and invaded Russia, the communists' gloves came off and, on 21 August 1941, Pierre Georges committed the first deliberate assassination, shooting a German naval officer on the Paris Metro – an act which was to provoke bitter reprisals.

Pierre Georges, AKA 'Colonel Fabien' of the FTP, who assassinated a German naval officer on the Paris Metro, 21 August 1941. (IWM MH11137)

From the outset of the occupation the Germans had a policy of taking hostages from sections of the population from which hostility might be expected. This practice was seen by the German High Command as a justified measure for maintaining order in occupied territories. The 'Code of Hostages', introduced in France on 30 September 1941, was a reaction to the incident of 21 August. On 22 August 1941 the German military commander of France, Karl von Stülpnagel, announced that, following the murder, all Frenchmen held in German custody could be considered hostages. If any further incident occurred, a number of these hostages would be shot. A list of these hostages was drawn up by the German military command, identifying those who could be executed immediately in the event of an incident.

To maximize the impact of these executions, the district chief was urged to select hostages 'belonging to a circle which is presumed to include the guilty'. In respect to the communists, the Germans made a point of placing former deputies and officials of the PCF at the top of the hostage lists. They would be followed by: intellectuals who had shown support for communism; persons who had proved themselves a threat by possessing arms or carrying out sabotage; and those who had collaborated in the distribution of leaflets. Following the same directives, a list of those prisoners with Gaullist sympathies was prepared. In all, each district was to have identified about 150 hostages, while 300–400 were chosen for Paris.

Regardless of the hostage programme the Feldkommandant of Nantes, Oberstleutnant Hotz, was assassinated on the morning of 20 October 1941. The German reaction was to order the execution of 50 hostages immediately and another 50 if the assassins had not been arrested before midnight on 23 October 1941. Soon after a separate shooting in Bordeaux, the local Feldkommandant asked for the arrest of 100 individuals known to sympathize with the communist or the Gaullist movements. Fifty were executed. These were the first of almost 30,000 executions.

It is difficult to assess to what extent the hostage shooting worked for or against the Resistance. On one hand the majority of French citizens must have wished the Resistance attacks would stop in order to prevent the killing of innocent hostages. On the other hand, the communists saw the German retribution as a recruitment tool and preached a message of 'an eye for eye'. French communists knew that the more trouble they caused, the fewer divisions could be transferred to the Russian front. Through the summer of 1941 the OS were transformed into a paramilitary group called the *Francs-Tireurs et Partisans Français* (French Snipers and Partisans; FTPF), or more commonly, the FTP. Unpalatable as it was to hear in the later era of the Cold War, many commentators pointed out that the communist partisans appeared by far the most eager to actually fight the Germans and were, in that sense, the most useful to the Allied cause.

The case of Resistance by French armed forces personnel is even more complex than that of the communists. Guerrilla war does not, as a rule, come naturally to trained, disciplined soldiers. Initially the army found itself in a sort of limbo. On the one hand it wanted revenge against Germany, but on the other it was steadfastly loyal to Pétain, who preached collaboration. Although the signs did not look good, many soldiers – and for that matter, almost all Frenchmen – hoped that the old marshal had a trick up his sleeve that would catch the Germans unawares. In the meantime, few soldiers wanted anything to do with the British, or de Gaulle and his 'Free French' – it must be remembered that any form of association invited the death penalty. In addition, the Germans were carefully watching all French officers for signs of recalcitrance. Anyone suspected of being or potentially becoming a part of the Resistance would have his or her family interned in Germany as a guarantee of loyalty.

While waiting for its resurrection, the French Army did at least try to hide some of its equipment from the Germans. Under the command of Colonel Vigier, officers secretly recruited reservist officers to hide anything from ammunition to tanks in their barns and cellars. When the Germans occupied the Free Zone in November 1942 and began disarming the Vichy army, significant numbers of soldiers at last began joining the Resistance. On 1 December 1942 the *Organisation de Résistance de l'Armée* (Army Resistance Organization; ORA) was formed by General Aubert Frère. Although Frère was arrested by the Gestapo in June 1943, ORA survived him and contributed to the liberation of France in 1944. It is important to know that ORA lent its support to a rival of de Gaulle, General Henri Giraud, who after escaping from captivity in Germany set up base in Algeria. It is also important to know that Giraud was preferred by the United States as a leader of the Free French. It is well known that President Roosevelt loathed Charles de Gaulle.

Perhaps the most active component in the army Resistance was its intelligence service – the *Deuxième Bureau*. The agency set up a commercial business in Lyons that served as a front for its German Section. Ignoring the terms of the armistice, this section continued to gather intelligence on Germany, which was passed to the British. The *Bureaux de Menées Antinationales* (Office of Anti-national Conspiracies) provided cover for the activities of the counter-espionage section, which continued to detect and arrest German agents.

One should never forget that throughout the occupation, the French intelligence service preserved the secret of how the German *Enigma* code had been broken. Before the war Polish intelligence had broken the *Enigma* and even built its own versions of the German enciphering machine. When the Germans made changes to *Enigma*, the Poles let Britain and France into their secret. After the Nazi invasion in 1939, the Polish team went to France to carry on their work and when France fell in 1940 they moved to the southern zone and became known as the Cadix team. Although a number of the group were captured, tortured and sent to concentration camps, none of them betrayed the *Enigma* secret.

Some intelligence officers attained high rank in the Resistance. Captain Henri Frenay formed *Combat*, one of the largest resistance movements, and then became a member of de Gaulle's provisional government. In the Occupied Zone, the *Deuxième Bureau*'s Lieutenant-Colonel Alfred Touny took command of the *Organisation Civile et Militaire* (Civil and Military Organization; OCM) after the arrest of its chief in December 1941. As its title suggests, the OCM was largely made up of reserve officers and civil servants and was thus well staffed to produce a steady stream of intelligence from the Occupied Zone to de Gaulle's Free French intelligence service in London.

This service was formed in October 1941 and was called the *Bureau Central de Renseignements et d'Action* (Central Office for Intelligence and Action; BCRA). It was commanded by André Dewavrin who used the *nom-de-guerre* 'Colonel Passy'. A former *Deuxième Bureau* officer, Passy ran the BCRA in an office in Duke Street, London. By 1944 the BCRA was producing an information sheet twice a day for the Allied intelligence community. One of Passy's key subordinates, Colonel Rémy, formed an important network in France called *Confrérie de Notre Dame* (Brotherhood of Notre Dame; CND). This organization produced a mass of pictures and maps used by the invasion planners. It also procured highly detailed construction plans of German coastal defences, the so-called 'Atlantic Wall'.

Allied to the BCRA – although often in competition with it – were the British secret services. Here the importance of the Allied secret services as a common denominator between the various Resistance movements should be clearly stated. Although it is perhaps unfashionable in France to admit it, without the direct intervention of the British and, later, the Americans, Resistance in France would have remained underfunded, poorly armed, rudderless and to a large degree parochial in scope.

On 19 July 1940 the British formed the SOE, a secret force that dropped agents behind enemy lines to stir up trouble, conduct sabotage, or, in Churchill's words, 'set Europe ablaze'. It is probably true to say that even if indigenous Resistance groups had not formed spontaneously of their own accord, the British would have created them. SOE's 'F' section was responsible for operations in France and was commanded by Maurice Buckmaster. Between March 1941 and September 1942, F Section alone included over 90 agent networks, or 'circuits' as they were known. The membership of these groups ranged from the singular (the *Tutor* circuit consisted of one man who was active for just a week) to the tens of thousands. Of these groups around 50 were still in action when reached by Allied soldiers in 1944, or when they ousted the Germans themselves – as in the case of the *Wheelwright* circuit, which liberated Toulouse. As support for de Gaulle began to increase in the Resistance, a separate Gaullist French section was formed under the initials 'FR'. After 1942 the SOE was joined by the American Office of Strategic Services (OSS), the forerunner of the modern Central Intelligence Agency (CIA).

It is also important to underline how much of the Resistance in France was not French at all. Resistance to Nazi occupation was a European phenomenon and not unique to France. In 1939 there were at least 2.5 million foreigners in France, mostly economic migrants who had come to take advantage of the labour shortage after World War I. Many of these had their own reasons for hating the Nazis. In the north of France, large numbers of Polish coal miners were active in the Resistance.

Perhaps as many as 60,000 Spanish exiles fought alongside the French Resistance, some forming their own groups, including the *Union Nacional Espanola* (Spanish National Union; UNE). In 1939 hundreds of thousands of Spanish had fled into France to avoid the fascist forces of General Franco after the fall of Catalonia. Although some attempts were made to repatriate them, by the end of the year there were still 250,000 exiles who were poorly housed in concentration camps. Despite this, many Spanish became fiercely loyal resisters, bringing considerable experience and knowledge of guerrilla warfare to the fight against the Nazi fascists. They were joined by Italians, Armenians, Romanians, Bulgarians, Hungarians, Czechs and citizens from the French colonies. Improbable as it may seem, there were even Germans in the French Resistance, with one notable band operating in the Cévennes region, made up of anti-fascists left over from the Spanish Civil War.

Before the war, the communist party had considerable support from France's large immigrant community. As early as 1923 the PCF had created the organization *Main d'Œuvre Immigrée* (lit. immigrant labour; MOI), to represent them. The membership of MOI increased in the 1930s with the arrival of those escaping fascism in their native countries. In April 1942 an armed wing of MOI (FPT-MOI) was formed in Paris under the command of the Jewish Bessarabian Boris Holban. In 1943 command of the Parisian FTP-MOI passed to the Armenian immigrant Missack Manouchain, who gave his name to the organization – *Groupe Manouchian*. Other significant FTP-MOI networks existed in Lyons (*Carmagnole*), Grenoble (*Liberté*) and Toulouse (*35e Brigade*).

There was also a large resistance network (classified 'F2' by the British) composed of Polish officers in France. Paris had been the seat of the Polish government-in-exile after 1939. Perhaps as many as 50,000 Poles fought with the French during the Battle of France and many were left behind after Dunkirk and the armistice. Perhaps the best known component of this network was *Interallié* commanded by Roman Czerniawski. Together with his number two, Mathilde Carré – codenamed *La Chatte* (the Cat) – Czerniawski passed information to Britain via a Polish organization based in Marseilles. Through Carré, Czerniawski also made contacts with several officers in the Vichy *Deuxième Bureau* who were active against the Germans.

In late 1940, Carré and Czerniawski moved to Paris, from where they established radio contact with Britain. It was here that the organization fell foul of the German intelligence service, or Abwehr. Carré was arrested and betrayed the organization to her captor, Abwehr Unterfeldwebel Hugo Bleicher. This led to the collapse of *Interallié* and the arrest of 100 agents including Czerniawski. Both Czerniawski and Carré agreed to go to Britain as double agents in February 1942, but Carré's duplicity was uncovered and she was interned for the remainder of the war. Czerniawski on the other hand defected to Britain's counter-espionage service, MI5. Under the codename *Brutus*, Czerniawski became one of the famous 'double-cross agents' responsible for feeding a series of elaborate deceptions to German High Command in the lead up to the D-Day landings in June 1944.

History should recognize the part played by women in the Resistance. Perhaps the most famous woman in the Resistance – certainly the most decorated – was Nancy Wake, a native of New Zealand who grew up in Australia and moved to France where she married a

A 'Jedburgh' radio operator (left) with members of the maquis. The two girls were only 16 at the time of the photograph and described as 'very brave'. Presumably they were used as messengers. The two figures on the right were brother and sister. The lorry they are leaning on was used for picking up containers on supply drops. (IWM HU62740)

French industrialist in 1939. Living in Marseilles, Wake joined the Resistance as a courier and worked on an Allied escape network. Hunted by the Germans, who called Wake the 'White Mouse', she escaped over the Pyrenees to Spain and travelled to Britain where she joined the SOE. Wake was then parachuted back into France and by April 1944 commanded a maquis of several thousand resisters. Clearly Nancy Wake is an exceptional example, but women were very active, working as organizers, couriers and the keepers of safe houses, writing for the underground press and carrying out attacks.

AN ARMY IN THE SHADOWS

Indigenous, civilian resistance began spontaneously. There were small acts of civil disobedience right from the start of German occupation. These individual acts, which ranged from giving wrong directions and malingering to minor acts of sabotage, were reinforced by the appearance of the underground press. Groups such as the *Musée de l'Homme* (Museum of Mankind) began to publish newspapers, which were distributed between trusted colleagues and friends. Other than advertising the existence of a Resistance, the clandestine press was a means of communicating the speeches of important figures like de Gaulle, Churchill and Roosevelt. It also helped spread the word of Allied successes or the abuses committed by German forces.

Alongside the underground press came the desire for organized, armed resistance. The memoirs of Resistance chief Henri Frenay reveal how in 1940 he began recruiting an organization by word of mouth. Frenay had drawn up a manifesto of his beliefs – namely that Germany would lose the war as Britain was still fighting fiercely and that it was only a matter of time before America joined them. France, he would say, needed to be ready for this hour. Whenever Frenay met someone, he would sound out their feelings about England and Germany. If the person appeared interested, Frenay would throw out a hook: 'Men are already gathering in the shadows. Will you join them?' If the reply was in the affirmative, Frenay would have a local resister get in touch with them. It was perhaps not the most secure means of recruiting, but in the early days the Gestapo was not active in the southern zone and *les flics* (the police) had yet to clamp down on them.

Once someone had been recruited into Frenay's network, he or she was passed through an induction service named ROP, which stood for *Recrutement, Organisation, Propagande*. Depending on the aptitude of the recruit, he would either remain with ROP as a reservist, or be transferred to the intelligence service or the *Choc* (Shock) – the paramilitary branch. Frenay explained how for security reasons these groups were organized into cells:

> The ROP and *Choc* were further divided into six-man and thirty-man cells. Each chief of a six-man cell only knew his five subordinates and his immediate supervisor in the larger, thirty-man cell. In turn the latter only knew the leaders of the five six-man cells placed under his orders. Above the thirty-man cells was the clandestine administrative superstructure…

Credited with unifying the internal Resistance under de Gaulle's Free French banner, Jean Moulin is one of the great French heroes of World War II. Apparently he wore the scarf to cover the scars of his suicide attempt when first held in captivity by the Germans. In 1940 they had arrested him after he refused to sign a false statement that Senegalese troops had committed an atrocity against French civilians. (IWM MH11145)

Similar groups began to spring up across France and it was a natural evolution for them to merge or at least cooperate when their interests converged. The chief promoter of unification was Jean Moulin, the pre-war government prefect at Chartres. Moulin identified three main Resistance groups in the southern zone. Although not seeing eye-to-eye on everything, these three groups shared many of the same goals and all of the same problems – namely a lack of money, no means of communicating with London and a dearth of equipment. Moulin decided to visit de Gaulle and lobby him on these issues.

Moulin reached Lisbon on 12 September 1941 and was taken by the British to London where he met de Gaulle on 25 October. De Gaulle agreed to help Moulin and made him his representative in France. As much as the Resistance needed help from London, de Gaulle needed the Resistance. If de Gaulle was recognized by the internal Resistance, it would lend him real political power with the Allied leadership. On the night of 2 January 1942, Moulin parachuted back into France with the aim of unifying the Resistance in de Gaulle's name.

Although much celebrated since, this mission was in fact a disaster waiting to happen. For secret organizations to survive they must decentralize and limit contact with each other. Although understanding the need to show unity, and accepting that de Gaulle was probably the best placed leadership candidate, many important resisters felt that de Gaulle, a military man, misunderstood the nature of the Resistance. The majority of civilians in the Resistance did not see themselves as soldiers, but, according to Frenay, were more like the *sans culottes* of the French Revolution – in other words, citizens in arms. However, to de Gaulle and his cohorts, the Resistance was seen as an embryonic military force, needing commanders, structures and all the trappings of a regular army.

As the FTP chief Charles Tillon wrote, the BCRA only appeared interested in drawing up lists of members, 'Yes, the Gaullist high command accounted for *résistants* like a collection of lead soldiers', he complained. This rejection of regimentation was shared by the *Libération* group's Emmanuel d'Astier de la Vigerie. When he met the BCRA chief, d'Astier was shown the BCRA's index system of known Resistance members. It comprised thousands of cards enclosed in huge metal filing cabinets, each detailing what was known about resisters and collaborators alike – very similar, d'Astier thought, to a police file.

The Secret Army

After a year of negotiation, the leaderships of the three main southern movements (*Combat, Franc-Tireur* and *Libération*) amalgamated on 26

January 1943 to form the *Mouvements Unis de Résistance* (United Resistance Movements; MUR – lit. wall). In addition to recognizing de Gaulle as leader, they agreed to merge their paramilitary branches to form the *Armée Secrète* (Secret Army; AS), which was placed under the independent command of General Delestraint (codename: *Vidal*), a former army commander of 1940.

Perhaps the biggest question facing the AS was how to incorporate the growing number of maquisards. Usually each no more than a dozen strong, maquis groups had been gathering in the Hautes-Alpes, the Cévennes, the Montagne Noire, Puy-de-Dôme and Corrèze. Frenay recalled:

> We established contact with them through our departmental and regional chiefs. Usually these little maquis voluntarily followed our instructions, in return for which they expected food, arms and ammunition... It seemed to me that these groups, which were now hiding out all over the French mountain country, might well be transformed into an awesome combat weapon. The *maquisards* were all young, all volunteers, all itching for action... It was up to us to organize them and give them a sense of their role in the struggle.

By 1 October 1943, the AS was a potent force with 241,350 members, although mostly unarmed. The AS followed the cell structure already used by *Combat*. The basic tactical group would be a *sixaines* (five men and a leader). Five *sixaines* would form a *trentaine* (thirty) under the command of a leader. Three *trentaines* would unite under a commander and a four-man staff (one deputy, four liaison agents) forming a 100-man unit or *centaine* (hundred – see Figure i).

Although some detachments – the *Groupes Francs* – would take immediate action, the bulk of the AS would remain living at home or in the maquis until called for on *Jour J* (D-Day). There was a genuine fear that if the AS attempted anything large before the Allied landings it would be quickly defeated by the Wehrmacht, as it had no heavy equipment. Instead the AS was told to concentrate on recruitment and the training of its members, waiting for a signal from London before commencing major operations.

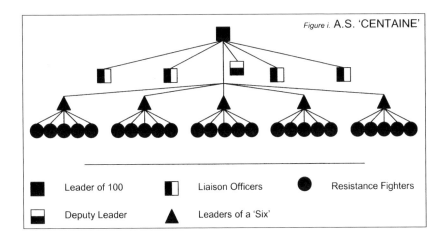

Figure i. A.S. 'CENTAINE'

| ■ | Leader of 100 | ▯ | Liaison Officers | ● | Resistance Fighters |
| ▭ | Deputy Leader | ▲ | Leaders of a 'Six' | | |

Elsewhere attempts had been made in 1943 to unite the various resistance groups in the occupied zones. Moulin secretly sent envoys into the northern zone locating such groups as *Libération-Nord*; the OCM; *Ceux de la Résistance* (Those of the Resistance; CDLR) and *Ceux de la Libération* (Those of the Liberation; CDLL). This led to the formation of the *Comité de Coordination de Zone Nord* (Coordination Committee of the Northern Zone; CCZN) on 26 March 1943. Then, on 27 May 1943 Moulin chaired the first meeting of the *Conseil National de la Résistance* (Nation Council of the Resistance; CNR) in Paris. This session included representatives from the majority of important Resistance movements: CDLL, CDLR, FN, *Libération-Nord*, OCM, *Combat*, *Franc-Tireur* and *Libération-Sud*. It also had representatives from the pre-war political parties and trade unions.

The CNR leadership soon encountered disaster. On 9 June 1943 General Delestraint was arrested by the Gestapo and sent to Dachau concentration camp. Suspecting treachery, Moulin called a meeting of AS chiefs on 21 June at Caluire near Lyons. Shortly after arriving in Lyons, Moulin received a message to meet Resistance leaders in a public garden. When he and several others arrived they found themselves surrounded and arrested by a Gestapo unit led by Klaus Barbie – the notorious 'Butcher of Lyons'. Throughout his ordeal, Moulin did not talk. Although never confirmed, it is believed Moulin was beaten into a coma and succumbed to his injuries on 8 July en route to a concentration camp. His body was sent to Paris where it was incinerated.

The FTP

Running parallel to the AS, by the end of 1943 the communist FTP had developed into a formidable partisan force operating in the northern and southern zones. Like the AS it was organized into small cells. Initially these were simple two- to three-man teams, but later the organization became much more complex (Figure ii). The basic building block of the FTP was the Combat Group, which comprised of seven men and a *chef de groupe* (group leader). For security and mobility, each group was divided into two teams of four men. The second team was commanded by an *adjoint* (assistant) to the *chef de groupe*. The members of a team or group would only assemble for an operation and would immediately disband after carrying it out. The hideouts of the individual men were kept secret from the *chef de groupe* in case he was captured.

Larger detachments could be formed by joining four combat groups together under the command of a *chef de détachement* who would be in communication with the higher echelons of the FTP. This leader would be assisted by a small staff comprising two *adjoints*, one of whom was responsible for recruitment, organization and morale and the other for intelligence gathering, the procurement and manufacture of weapons, gathering rations and health issues. When three or four detachments operated together in the same area they formed a company. This was especially the case after 1943 because of the increased recruitment of STO *réfractaires*.

In some cases, two or three companies would go on to form battalions, but this formation would only assemble just prior to action. Otherwise the FTP preferred to keep its men dispersed. A company of 100–150 men would be spread over four or five *cantonnements* (quarters)

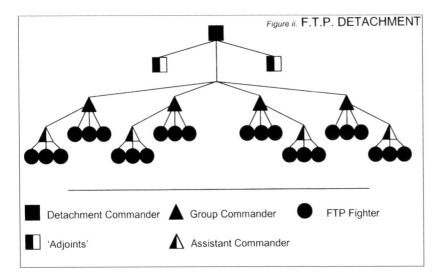

Figure ii. F.T.P. DETACHMENT

| ■ Detachment Commander | ▲ Group Commander | ● FTP Fighter |
| ◧ 'Adjoints' | ◮ Assistant Commander | |

with a maximum of 30 men in each. These *cantonnements* were sited far away enough for them not to be surrounded, but close enough for them to be mutually supporting.

Above battalion level, the FTP was organized as follows. A *Comité Militaire Régional* (Regional Military Committee; CMR) was responsible for a region comprising one, or sometimes two, *départements* of France. Several 'regions' formed an *inter-région* directed by a *Comité Militaire Inter-Régional* (Inter-Regional Military Committee; CMRI). The CMRIs were directed by a *Comité Militaire National* (National Military Committee; CMN). The wishes of the CMN were made known at local level by a sub-regional commandant (sub-regions were a group of several *inter-régions*). Operations beyond the German-held line of demarcation into the southern zone were overseen by a special delegation, the *Comité Militaire de Zone Sud* (Military Committee of the Southern Zone; CMZ).

Each of these echelons was supported by a 'triangle' of three officers. The *commissaire aux effectifs* (commissioner for manpower; CE) was principally responsible for recruitment and communication between the various groups. The *commissaire aux operations* (CO) was responsible for planning operations and training the men for combat, while the *commissaire technique* (technical commissioner; CT) was concerned with arms, intelligence and health.

To formalize membership, the FTP introduced an *engagement d'honneur* – a code of conduct for members. By signing this code, FTP members made a formal pledge to serve honourably until the complete liberation of French territory. The FTP were, the code stated, the advanced guard on French soil of the *France Combattante* (Fighting French) armies of both General de Gaulle and General Giraud. The soldiers pledged to fight with all their strength, to obey commands and show discipline, and to come to the aid of comrades in danger. They were to take an active part in recruitment; submit themselves for training and instruction; study the art of war and weapons handling; and maintain their readiness for action. They were instructed to take particular care within the city or countryside they operated in, to pass unperceived and to restrict their visits. Above all, they were to be well behaved and to show gratitude to those who assisted them.

From the security aspect, members pledged to retain absolute secrecy regarding the FTP and to resist all threats and tortures designed to make them talk about persons or operations, both previous and forthcoming. They were to avenge all crimes against 'patriots' committed by the enemy and so-called 'French' police officers in their pay. The death penalty was to be carried out immediately against informers and anyone trying to prevent this was to be seen as an accomplice and also punished.

The FTP's strategy was to strike at the enemy and then vanish. They drew their inspiration from French history, remembering how royalist Chouan rebels in Brittany had waged a guerrilla war during the Revolution and how the Spanish guerrillas had fought against Napoleon. Equally they were inspired by and took their name from the *Franc-tireur* irregulars of the Franco-Prussian War, who fought behind German lines at considerable cost. The FTP groups also benefited from the experience of those who had fought in the International Brigade in the Spanish Civil War.

In the early days, FTP groups were urban guerrillas. Their attacks were brutally efficient. For example, a grenade thrown into the back of a German lorry carrying 30 men exploded with terrible effect; a German detachment marching along the street had two grenades thrown at it; a grenade was thrown into a restaurant frequented by German officers; a German *Soldatenheim* (recuperation centre) was blown up; mines exploded under passing German convoys; trains were attacked, troops machine-gunned and hotels bombed; grenades were thrown at an SS detachment on the Champs Élysées. All these attacks meant the

Maquis in action. The figure in the foreground is about to throw a grenade while his comrades lay down covering fire. (IWM MH27379)

Germans could not walk the streets unguarded and they also showed the population that the Nazis were not the supermen they believed themselves to be. The FTP put out a rallying cry for everyone to get a German: '*Chacun son Boche*'.

The FFI command structure

The third main Resistance group, the ORA, which backed General Giraud, did not join the CNR. However, in October 1943, after an accord between generals de Gaulle and Giraud, ORA and AS joined forces. Through further negotiations an agreement was also reached with the FTP. Although disagreeing with the tactics adopted by the Gaullist groups, the FTP thought it beneficial for the Resistance to have commanders who sat alongside the Allied leadership planning the invasion. More than anything, the FTP erroneously believed this would lead to them receiving more supplies and weapons. Therefore, after 29 December 1943, AS and FTP activities were coordinated by COMAC, the acronym of the *Comité Militaire d'Action*, a three-man body that in itself was answerable to the CNR, which by that stage had become increasingly dominated by communists. However, it should be stated that in reality the FTP went its own way and should be considered as an independent group.

In February 1944, the combined forces of the Resistance became known as the *Forces Françaises de l'Intérieur* (French Forces of the Interior; FFI). On 23 March 1944, the FFI was placed under the command of General Pierre Koenig who had risen to prominence as a commander of Free French troops. Koenig was sent from Algeria to place himself and the Resistance at Eisenhower's disposal. He was also to lobby Supreme Headquarters Allied Expeditionary Force (SHAEF) to have all the agencies dealing with the FFI brought under one roof – a body that would come to be known as *État Major des Forces Françaises de l'Intérieur* (General Staff, French Forces of the Interior; EMFFI).

Unfortunately for Koenig, the Anglo-Americans had no intention of revealing anything about the forthcoming invasion to the Free French. According to William Casey, an OSS officer and future CIA chief, British and American commanders at SHAEF never fully trusted the Free French or the Resistance movements, which appeared more tied up with domestic political agendas than defeating Germany. No part of the planning would rely on the Resistance and any assistance provided by it subsequent to the invasion would be treated as a bonus. Even de Gaulle was not privy to the invasion plans. He was only informed by Churchill on the evening of 4 June as a matter of protocol because Free French troops would be among the first wave sent over. De Gaulle never forgave his allies for this slight.

However, once the invasion took place and there was no longer any secrecy over its timing, on 9 June SHAEF reached an agreement – subject to Eisenhower's approval – that Koenig would assume command of the FFI, but that he would be under Eisenhower's command. In reply, the French authorities in Algeria stipulated that the FFI were now part of the French Army and were to be treated as regular soldiers. Official ranks were conferred on FFI officers. The commanders of 30 men became *sous-lieutenants*; commanders of 100 men became *lieutenants*; commanders of 300 became *capitaines*; leaders of 1,000 men and departmental commanders became *commandants*; leaders of 2,000 men and commanders of military regions became *lieutenant-colonels*. Holders of these ranks were authorized to wear the appropriate insignia and would be recognized as legitimate military personnel by Allied troops. Unfortunately, this did little to stop the Germans from shooting them if captured. The German commander in the theatre, Gerd von Rundstedt, had put out a communiqué on 12 June declaring that FFI troops would be treated as partisans.

On 23 June Eisenhower endorsed Koenig's command. Initially Koenig was required to issue his directives to the Resistance through an organization known as the Special Force Headquarters (SFHQ), a body composed of SOE and the Special Operations (SO) branch of OSS. However, it was agreed that Koenig would gradually relieve the SFHQ of its responsibilities in connection with the French Resistance, a change that took place on 21 August. Directives were issued by the EMFFI, now in control of not just the FFI, but also the agents formerly run by the BCRA and SOE's F and RF sections. It also became responsible for a number of Allied Special Forces teams that had been working with the Resistance since D-Day.

To complement the existing BCRA/SOE operatives working in France on the eve of the invasion, uniformed Allied soldiers were parachuted in to make contact with the local maquis groups, assess their strengths and requirements and put them inside the Allied command structure. These liaison teams were codenamed 'Jedburghs'. Each 'Jed' was made up of a commander, his deputy and a radio operator. One of the officers would be French, the other American or British; the radio operator would be an NCO. In all, 300 volunteers were trained and organized into 93 teams, all of which were sent into France on or after D-Day. They were complemented by a number of heavily armed OSS Operational Groups (OGs) which also came under EMFFI command.

LIVING CLANDESTINELY

One cannot overstate the level of risk faced by all members of the Resistance, whatever their affiliation or rank. Theirs was an uncommon bravery very different from that shown by soldiers of previous wars fought by the French. Unlike their ancestors who had fought at Austerlitz and Verdun, resisters often found themselves isolated from their comrades. Instead they relied on their will-power, inventiveness, boldness, cheek and, above all, their luck.

A good resister had to melt into the background and pass unobserved. To stand out would invite suspicion and scrutiny. Silence was golden; not just under the spotlight of interrogation, but every single day. For resisters to come together, or even simply to avoid arrest and survive, elaborate precautions were called for in all facets of life. The slightest lapse of attention, the smallest detail overlooked, and the resister was in grave danger. For many the tension of this life became so unbearable that capture seemed, albeit temporarily, a relief.

Agents about to leave for France were checked to ensure their clothes did not have British labels or the wrong style of cut. The earliest agents were kitted out from clothes taken from refugees. Another stupid

A maquis garage. Using vehicles for transport was against every rule of clandestine living and bicycles were the preferred method of movement. However, using back roads maquis groups would drive out of their hiding places with Stens and Bren guns pointing out of every opening and cover the large distances between different groups. (IWM MH11131)

mistake was to use handkerchiefs or hats with initials sewn into them which were different from the initials of the resister's assumed name. Consecutive nights were rarely spent in the same place. In cities resisters sent their liaison officers out to find safe houses among trusty friends who were not engaged in illegal activities themselves. By agreeing to shelter resisters, the owners of safe houses ran terrible risks if captured. Nancy Wake was almost caught out when a neighbour heard her toilet being flushed more frequently at night than usual. Wake told the inquisitive neighbour she had a stomach ache, when in reality the house was full of careless Allied evaders.

Their lives were the stuff of spy novels. Meetings usually took place in busy public areas. The Germans often sent their spies to be on the lookout for strangers, so high-traffic areas were vital. Punctuality was the key to a successful meeting. German spies would also be watching out for people who seemed to be waiting for someone. If the resister or agent arrived at the rendezvous and was not met as planned, it was advisable to keep walking in case the contact had been arrested and the Gestapo were watching from a nearby building. SOE agent Yeo-Thomas ignored this rule and was picked up by the Gestapo – his contact was not at the Metro station as planned, so he walked a circuit and came back to the same spot. This gave him away and he ended up in Buchenwald concentration camp.

False papers were key to a resister's survival. These included not just a good fake ID card, but the whole range of documents one might expect a French civilian to hold during the occupation. Official documentation included ration card and coupons, tobacco vouchers (whether you smoked or not), work permits, travel permits, passes to certain restricted areas and also exemption certificates from the labour programmes, release certificates for former prisoners of war, medical certificates and so on – the list was almost endless. In order to produce the required number of forgeries, both the Resistance and SOE needed to recruit forgers. In addition to printing presses, the forgers themselves

Fake identity used by SOE agent Peter Churchill on his missions to France. Agents and Resistance leaders would often use a number of false identities and would learn complex cover stories to back them up. However, being caught with more than one ID card was in itself an admission of guilt. In this case Churchill could do nothing when betrayed by Abwehr spies who infiltrated the Resistance. (IWM HU66775)

required rubber stamps, sample signatures, the correct type of postage stamps and accurate addresses. According to Frenay, his men would dress a couple of agents up with fake police ID cards. These two men would walk around looking for someone who looked similar to the person requiring the fake ID. They would stop that person, ask for his papers and make a copy of the details on the card under the pretext of investigating them. Armed with the person's details they would go to a forger and hijack his or her identity.

A classic feature of Resistance life was listening to illicit radio messages broadcast by the BBC. Despite German attempts to drown transmissions with a wall of ululating static, each night at 9.15pm coded 'personal messages' were sent out by the BBC for the Resistance. The messages were always preceded by a signature tune – the first four notes of Beethoven's Fifth Symphony. The four notes sounded like Morse code for the letter 'V' and symbolized 'Victory'.

Several memoirs speak of Resistance members and British agents proving their credentials by asking locals to give them a message, which would be broadcast by the BBC that night. This demonstrated that the agent had a means of communicating with London and, more importantly, that he was not a double-agent planted by the Gestapo or *Milice*. The messages were short and normally meaningless outside of the group that had chosen it – for example: '*Yvette aime les grosses carottes*' (Yvette likes large carrots), which was the call sign for one group to receive a parachute drop.

Receiving messages from the BBC was one thing, but resisters needed a means of transmitting their requirements to London. The first contacts were made by intrepid individuals who travelled to Britain via Spain or by boat across the Channel. Later, some resisters were brought to London in a 'spy taxi' – one of the RAF's Lysander aircraft. However, although personal contact was desirable and even necessary, it was too slow. Whether supported by de Gaulle's BCRA or the British SOE, a Resistance group that was unable to contact London by radio was severely limited in its means of securing money, arms and other supplies. There was a lot of reliance on the SOE for providing radio operators to the Resistance. In May 1941 there were just two SOE stations operating in France for F Section. By August 1944 this number had risen to 53 stations.

The Germans had some impressive radio-detecting equipment available in the fight against the Resistance movements in occupied Europe. When a radio transmission appeared to come from an unauthorized source its position was triangulated from stations in Paris, Brittany, Ausburg and Nuremberg to an accuracy of within about 16km (10 miles). The local German operations centre would quickly send out

The nerve-wracking life of a clandestine radio operator. While the 'pianist' sends out his message in morse code, his colleague keeps watch at the window for the arrival of suspicious vehicles – in particular a black Citroën 'Traction-Avant', the preferred choice of Gestapo agents. (IWM MH27378)

A maquis wireless post operated by a soldier from the 3e Régiment Chasseurs Parachutistes (RCP) operating in Brittany after D-Day. Radios were the life blood of the maquis and it was vital for them to listen out for the 'personal messages' broadcast by the BBC. (IWM MH112339)

Table A

	P	A	R	I	S
a	12	1	10	19	9
b	13	2	11	20	10
c	14	3	12	21	11
d	15	4	13	22	12
e	16	5	14	23	13
f	17	6	15	24	14
g	18	7	16	25	15
h	19	8	17	26	16
i	20	9	18	1	17
j	21	10	19	2	18
k	22	11	20	3	19
l	23	12	21	4	20
m	24	13	22	5	21
n	25	14	23	6	22
o	26	15	24	7	23
p	1	16	25	8	24
q	2	17	26	9	25
r	3	18	1	10	26
s	4	19	2	11	1
t	5	20	3	12	2
u	6	21	4	13	3
v	7	22	5	14	4
w	8	23	6	15	5
x	9	24	7	16	6
y	10	25	8	17	7
z	11	26	9	18	8

Table B

P	A	R	I	S
r	e	n	d	e
z	v	o	u	s
c	e	s	o	i
r	c	h	e	z
h	e	n	r	i

Table C

P	A	R	I	S
3	5	23	22	13
11	22	24	13	1
14	5	2	7	17
3	3	17	23	3
19	5	23	10	17

vehicles equipped with receivers. Even if the clandestine receiver had stopped transmitting, a reply would soon be sent from London, potentially putting the Resistance radio operator back on the air. Although it is unlikely that the German secret service men would capture the radio operator first time off, if he was unwise enough to continue transmitting from the same hideout, night after night, the net would soon close in.

Then there were the codes. Only a fool would broadcast an 'open' message over airwaves that were constantly dissected by the German secret services. Much is made of the Allies' successes with the code-breaking establishment at Bletchley Park, but the Germans were no slouches in this field either. There were many codes and ciphers used by the Resistance, but a good, simple example is given by Guillain de Bénouville. The agent was told to remember a keyword upon which the cipher would be based. De Bénouville was given the codeword CHAMONIX, but, for simplicity, here we will use PARIS. Using this keyword, agents could quickly construct what code-breakers call a polyalphabetic cipher. Using the keyword 'PARIS' the agent would draw a grid like that of Table A. Seeing that 'P' was the first letter of the key, he would insert the number '1' by 'P' in the first column. In the next column he would write the number '1' next to the letter 'A' and so on.

Using this method, if our resister wanted to send the message '*rendez-vous ce soir chez Henri*' (meeting tonight at Henri's), he would draw another grid with P-A-R-I-S along the top and write the message shown in Table B.

He would then use his table to work out the values of each letter. The recipient – provided he knew the keyword – would then work backwards, drawing out a grid with P-A-R-I-S across the top with the numbers written as shown in Table C. He would then draw his own version of Table A and decipher the message.

If this message was intercepted without the keyword there would be little clue where to begin. If the group believed its keyword was in any way compromised, it was easy enough to change the keyword and thus the entire cipher would change.

As an additional precaution the radio operator would also give a security code to indicate that he was not transmitting under duress. When radio operators were captured the first thing on the mind of the Germans was to try to turn them into double agents and force them to carry on sending false transmissions to London.

Arrest and captivity

In the modern era soldiers have come to expect reasonably fair treatment if captured or injured in battle. Unfortunately, members of the Resistance were categorized not as soldiers, but as terrorists and outlaws. If caught alive they could expect little pity, unless of course they were radio operators who offered to be turned, or who quickly offered to become stool pigeons and betray their comrades.

The accounts of surviving prisoners all indicate the inhumanity of their treatment. They were kept on starvation rations of tainted food, were held in overcrowded cells infested with lice, fleas and bed-bugs, and were beaten or placed in solitary confinement. Torture was routinely used, even if, as was often the case, the interrogators had no clear idea of the information they wanted. It is believed that 40,000 Frenchmen died in French prisons that the Germans had requisitioned.

Evidence at the Nuremberg trials described an array of barbarous methods. Victims were often shackled or suspended from the ceiling and beaten or kicked until they fainted, only to be roused by a bucket of water in the face, whereupon the beating would resume. Electric shocks were administered: a wire was attached to the foot and another wire placed at different parts of the body. Some had their legs burned by a blow-torch, or were attacked by police dogs. One victim remembered being shut in a sort of coffin for hours at a time with just a few holes in the lid to breathe through. Many were lashed by ox-hide whips or were hit with hammers or other heavy objects, while others had their heads squeezed in vices. Many were subjected to the *baignoire* (bath-tub). Here the victim was forcibly submerged in a bathtub filled with freezing water and held under until at the point of drowning. At the last second he would be pulled out, questioned, abused and pushed back under until he agreed to talk. If all that failed the Germans would target the victim's family and loved ones. All but the strongest would talk once the interrogators threatened to have their fiancée or sister sent to a German army brothel.

Women were subjected to the same ordeals and faced beatings as severe as the men. One survivor, Madame Sindemans, recounted how she was arrested in Paris on 24 February 1944 after soldiers found her carrying stolen identification cards and German work passes. 'Immediately, they handcuffed me and took me to be interrogated', she recalled. 'Getting no reply, they slapped me in the face with such force that I fell from my chair. Then they whipped me with a rubber hose, full in the face. This interrogation began at 10 o'clock in the morning and ended at 11 o'clock that night. I must tell you that I had been pregnant for three months.'

French SOE agent Odette Sansom survived months of interrogation by the Gestapo in Paris's Fresnes prison. In an interview after the war she recalled how she mentally resisted her tormentors:

In those places the only thing one could try to keep was a certain dignity. There was nothing else. And one could have a little dignity and try to prove that one had a little spirit and, I suppose, that kept one going. When everything was too difficult, too bad, then one was inspired by so many things – people; perhaps a phrase one would remember that one had heard a long time before, or even a piece of poetry or a piece of music.

A Gestapo cell, Bordeaux, with graffiti on the wall encouraging future inmates to take courage. Under interrogation even the toughest could expect to break some time and many chose to commit suicide before this could happen. One senior Resistance figure, Pierre Brossolette, was captured by the Gestapo, who did not realize the significance of their arrest. Brossolette had a distinctive streak of white hair, which he had dyed, but which would no doubt soon grow through. Before this could happen he jumped from a sixth-floor window in the Gestapo's Paris headquarters on the Avenue Foch. (IWM R.1758)

In June 1943 Odette Sansom was transported to Ravensbruck concentration camp in Germany – an ordeal she managed to survive. The conditions faced by the inmates of Nazi concentration camps need no introduction here. Members of the Resistance were classed as *Nacht und Nebel* (Night and Fog) prisoners. These were the prisoners Hitler wanted simply to disappear. Of the 200,000 French citizens deported to concentration camps, perhaps as many as 75,000 were also members of the Resistance. It is estimated that half of French inmates did not survive.

Chances to escape before deportation or execution were rare, but one episode stands out as among the most audacious jail breaks in history. A number of high-profile Resistance fighters were being held at Amiens prison and many were scheduled for execution on 20 February 1944. A plan was hatched by Dominique Ponchardier – founder member of the *Sosies* intelligence network – to get the RAF to breach the prison walls with a low-level attack, allowing the prisoners to escape and rejoin the Resistance in the build up to D-Day. Among the 700 inmates was Raymond Vivant, the sub-prefect of Abbeville who had been arrested by the Gestapo on 12 February on suspicion of Resistance activities. On the morning of 18 February, Vivant was preparing for his lunch when he heard the drone of aircraft engines followed by a loud explosion:

> I thought initially that a German plane had just crashed very close to us, and I began to delight in this when a succession of explosions resounded. Out of instinct, I leaned myself against an angle of my cell, while the panes of the fanlight flew in fragments. I saw the wall on the left side split open abruptly and a cloud dust invaded my cell. I remained motionless, awaiting the end of the explosions, believing that an aerial combat had taken place above our heads. 'Some planes have crashed with their bomb loads,' I thought. But, as soon as the cloud of dust dissipated, I saw that the door was torn from its hinges. The long corridor which served my cell, on both floors of the prison, an immense heap of stones, had been replaced by a cluster of smoking debris! On the right-hand side, the other part of the prison appeared intact. But, to the left, with inexpressible joy, I saw the countryside, covered with snow, extending to infinity. A large breach had been opened in the high surrounding wall…

Needless to say, Vivant ran for his life and was one of 258 prisoners who escaped. Unfortunately, 102 prisoners were killed and 74 wounded in the attack by RAF Mosquito bombers, but almost everyone involved with the Resistance agreed it was a price worth paying.

LIFE IN THE MAQUIS

A great many resisters in the AS or FTP were able to remain at home after recruitment and carry on with their normal routines, waiting for the call on D-Day. However, for the *réfractaires* on the run from the authorities, staying at home was simply not an option. They had to find shelter and thus took to the maquis in large numbers.

France possesses many mountainous and inhospitable regions, often thickly covered with woodland or dense shrub. Such terrain made the perfect hiding place for *réfractaires* because unless the Germans committed thousands of troops to combing an area from all directions simultaneously, it was quite possible to remain hidden and evade capture. The Germans did utilize spotter planes, but aerial reconnaissance was hampered by the tree canopy that afforded the maquis cover, provided they were careful with their cooking fires.

A number of SOE agents parachuting into France for the first time were appalled by the lax security they found. Bored out of their minds, maquisards might wander down into nearby villages and drink in cafés where, no doubt to impress the local mademoiselles, they would brag about their membership in the Resistance. Informants were always a problem. Although the maquis often received loyal and steadfast support from local villagers and farmers, there were collaborators waiting to betray them. Of course, some of the maquis groups did themselves no favours with their rowdy conduct and were often labelled as gangsters. One of the most common causes of friction between maquis and village came from the procurement of cigarettes. More than one source mentions how when funds ran low the maquis would hold up the local tobacconist kiosk on delivery day. This sort of behaviour only alienated the maquis and led to people informing on them.

The worst security issue facing the maquis was the danger of being infiltrated by a spy. As taking to the maquis became more commonplace, it was easier for the Germans and *Milice* to infiltrate agents into the maquis. Once there was a spy in the camp it often spelled death for the group. After D-Day, when some maquis groups received thousands of recruits, just one spy could wreck everything. Needless to say, if the maquis caught a spy in their midst, justice was swift and brutal. The unlucky spy could expect nothing more than a shovel with which to dig his own grave and a bullet in the back of the head.

With no clear direction from the Vatican and in the face of Nazi Teutonic paganism, some French priests took to the maquis. Here we have Father Bernard giving an Easter Mass to an FTP maquis. (IWM MH11176)

More than anything, when cut off from their families and homes, the members of a maquis needed to be told that their sacrifice was both worth it and necessary. Be it the BBC, or, as in this case, a sympathetic priest, such boosts were vital to keep the morale of a maquis intact. (IWM MH11177)

Chores in a maquis cookhouse. Notice that the cooking is not done over a roaring fire, which would produce too much smoke and attract attention. Also note that canopies have been thrown up to offer shelter both from the elements and against German spotter planes. (IWM MH11130)

Captured maquisards were expected to reveal the location of their hidden base under extreme duress. If a member of the maquis was captured or gave himself up, his colleagues had no more than 24 hours to break camp and find a new hideout. That was the rule to all resisters if captured – whatever they did to you, hold out for 24 hours to give your colleagues a chance to run.

Returning to the maquis itself, the typical encampment before D-Day would hold a small group of young men effectively living rough under the stars. Outdoor life presents a number of issues. There is the need for shelter, for food and water, for fire to cook on and utensils to cook with; latrines need to be dug and, perhaps most importantly, safe storage must be provided for weapons and equipment. Most *réfractaires* were young men from the towns and cities with no military experience or training. Some made tents, others made log cabins and bivouacs. Another thing that struck Allied agents was how parachutes from supply drops were not incinerated as ordered, but used for practically every conceivable use. The nylon canopies were used to make tents, sheets and soft bedding for men to put their sleeping bags on.

To alleviate the discomfort of men going to the maquis, the underground press printed advice on what items to bring. One such article warned potential maquisards of the hardships they would be forced to endure for the duration of hostilities. They were told to forget about being paid or making any contact with their families while serving. They were to bring their papers, even false ones, providing they were perfectly in order. Most importantly they were to bring ration coupons. In terms of personal kit they were instructed to bring two shirts, two pairs of drawers, two pairs of woollen socks, a sweater, a muffler, a pullover, a woollen blanket, a spare pair of shoes, laces, wire, needles, spare buttons, safety pins, soap, a water bottle, mess tin, knife, spoon, fork, cup, torch, compass, sleeping bag, beret, waterproof coat

and a good pair of studded shoes. If they could lay their hands on a weapon, all the better.

Generally speaking, there is little to say on the actual appearance of maquisards in terms of uniforms. However, the following descriptions of maquis groups in 1944 are useful. SOE agent George Millar gave his first impression of the maquis on landing: 'I saw in the moonlight that some wore ordinary civilian clothes, while others were dressed in odd scraps of rags, old uniforms, and leather coats that I had learned to expect in the maquis.' Landing in the Morvan region, SAS officer Ian Wellsted gave the following description of a maquis band:

> It was hard to tell what they had been before the German labour laws threw them all together in the depths of the wild woods. Some had been shopkeepers, artisans, young sons of wealthy parents. Others were scum of the gutter and many were soldiers. Now, however, all were much the same. All wore the clothes, and many still the wooden clogs, of peasants. Some lucky ones had scraps of uniform and British battledress, but predominantly their clothes consisted of drab coloured shirts, blue overall trousers and German field boots, whose owners no doubt had ceased to require them for obvious reasons. They wore neither brassards nor regular uniform of any kind. The only distinguishable difference between the men of the Maquis and the men of the country from which they had sprung was the pistol cocked aggressively from the trouser tops, the rifle on the shoulder, the Sten on the back or the string of grenades depending from the belt.

Against these freewheeling examples, a more uniformed representation is shown in the Museum of the Order of Liberation in

Paris. This costume shows a dark green, hooded jacket of the type issued to young men on the *Chantiers de Jeunesse* (Youth Work Farms). These were part of a government programme where young Frenchmen were obliged to spend eight months in a *chantier*. Publicly it was a way of providing work and distraction for those reaching military age and, in many cases, whose fathers were absent, held prisoner in Germany. The real function of the *chantiers* was to provide 'the rudiments of discipline, hygiene and endurance' normally found in National Service. It also allowed the army to gather the statistics previously collected by recruitment bureaus. While on the *chantiers* some individuals did go on to join the maquis. Also, *chantier* depots were a good source of supplies for maquis raiding parties. With the museum figure in question, the *chantier* insignia was replaced by a Cross of Lorraine symbol. The rest of the uniform consisted of army boots, gaiters, British army trousers, leather gloves and was finished with a captured German army belt.

SUPPLY DROPS

USAAF B-17 Flying Fortresses drop supply containers to the maquis in Vercors. Normally parachutages occurred at night, so this photo gives a unique perspective on the process. (IWM EA34185)

The biggest problem facing the Resistance was supply. Although the Resistance within the French Army had begun concealing weapons in 1940, they were loath to share them. Equally, although the SOE and BCRA lobbied the British and American governments for weapons drops, very little was initially done. SHAEF's deep-seated distrust of the Resistance meant the French received very little in terms of arms and equipment through parachute drops. The French were considered less of a priority than Italian or Yugoslav partisans and some Allied leaders even feared that if the French were provided with weapons the various groups might use them against each other.

Even if weapons were made available, there was still the problem of delivery. Allied air marshals were reluctant to divert planes from dropping bombs on Germany to supplying the Resistance, although evidence suggested that sabotage on the ground was far more effective than aerial bombardment. The stormy winter of 1943–44 delayed many SOE drops, but more than bad weather, a lack of aircraft hampered efforts to supply the Resistance with arms. At the time there were only 23 Halifax bombers assigned to cover clandestine operations across the whole continent. After lobbying by the Resistance and SOE, in January Winston Churchill ordered that an additional 35 British aircraft be made available for arming maquis groups. Accordingly, supply drops in February increased 173 per cent, although the target had been a 300 per cent rise – bad weather again intervened. In April there were 331 drops; in May, 531; and in June, 866. Additional drops were made by the SOE's

Maquisard, 1944

The passage into Spain

B

A Lysander pickup

c

BEURRE · OEUFS · FROMAGES

CREME
FOUETTÉE

907 BO 2

D

Gestapo arrest, 1943

Resistance arms

E

Arms and containers

Plan Tortue

G

Resistance and the SAS.

H

American cousin, OSS, which was belatedly given support by the USAAF in January 1944.

The AS needed a huge number of weapons. For each group of six men it calculated a minimum of two submachine guns, two automatic pistols and 12 grenades. Furthermore, each submachine gun would need an initial 300 rounds, with a further ten cartridges per month. Automatic pistols required 25 cartridges initially, with a further five per month supplied afterwards. As shown in Table D, the requirements were enormous.

The principal weapon dropped to the maquis was the Sten gun. This was a mass-produced British submachine gun that was easy to use and could be broken down and hidden quite easily. It was not very accurate and was extremely loud when used, but it was cheap to produce. It was designed to fire the 9mm Parabellum round, which was very common on the Continent. Later in the war, the Sten was often replaced by the American M3 'Greasegun'. Pistols were sent by the thousand, but resisters preferred the American Browning automatic to the British Webley revolver. Above all, Resistance fighters wanted rifles. When British Lee-Enfields were dropped, these allowed the maquis to reply to the German Mauser. Bren guns were also particularly coveted. Again, as American involvement increased, so the M1 Carbine began to be supplied. Other weapons included American Bazookas, or the British

Table D – armament requirements 1943

	Groupes Francs	Armée Secrète
Effectives (unarmed)	54,000	127,000
Effectives (armed)	16,000	-
Submachine guns	18,000	42,350
Automatic pistols	18,000	42,350
Light machine guns	250	-
Heavy machine guns	600	-
Rocket launchers	100	-
Hand grenades	140,000	254,000
Carbines	250	-
Explosives	40 tonnes per month	-

Contents of a sabotage container, including hand grenades, plastic explosives, detonators, a wrench used for loosening rails, a selection of pistols, a commando knife and (bottom right) what appears to be a spring-loaded, telescopic cosh. (IWM R354)

Maquisards receiving an arms drop gather up parachutes and prepare the containers for transport. (IWM HU41895)

PIAT anti-tank weapon, both of which gave the Resistance some power in attacking vehicles and emplacements. The Resistance also received its sabotage material from the air, along with banknotes and field dressings. Those rare unfilled spaces in the containers were packed with treats such as cigarettes and chocolate.

Weapons were dropped by parachute in large, heavy, cylindrical containers. The 'Type C' container was approximately 1.7m (5ft 7in.) in length with a diameter of 0.35m (1ft 2in.). It could be divided into three compartments by inserting wooden disks inside, depending on the requirements of the load. The 'Type H' container was in fact five

Stunning picture of maquisards in Vercors transporting parachute containers back to their encampment. (IWM MH11163)

Table E

	LOAD A			LOAD B			LOAD C			LOAD D		
Number of containers in drop	12	15	18	12	15	18	12	15	18	12	15	18
Brens + 1,000 rounds per gun	6	6	6	-	-	-	-	-	-	8	8	8
Rifles + 150 rounds per gun	36	36	36	9	9	9	-	-	-	9	18	18
Stens + 300 rounds per gun	27	27	27	11	11	11	-	-	-	-	-	-
Pistols + 50 rounds per gun	5	5	5	-	-	-	-	-	-	-	-	-
Mills grenades	40	40	40	-	-	-	-	-	-	-	-	-
Gammon grenades	12	12	12	-	-	-	-	-	-	-	-	-
Field dressings	156	384	612	660	888	1,116	882	1,110	1,338	234	78	156
9mm Parabellum	6,600	13,200	19,800	13,200	19,800	26,400	19,800	6,600	660	-	-	-
.303 carton rounds	3,168	6,436	6,436	22,176	28,612	35,048	28,512	26,400	6,436	9,504	3,168	6,436
Empty Bren magazines	68	108	148	140	180	220	180	220	260	124	144	184
Empty Sten magazines	100	120	140	40	60	80	60	80	100	-	-	-
Explosives and accessories	-	70kg (145lb)	70kg (145lb)	70kg (145lb)	70kg (145lb)	70kg (145lb)	-	-	-	70kg (145lb)	132kg (290lb)	132kg (290lb)
Bazookas + 14 rockets each*	-	-	-	-	-	-	-	-	-	4	4	4
Bazooka rockets	-	-	-	-	-	-	-	-	-	40	40	80

*Could be substituted with British PIAT anti-tank weapons and ammunition

separate cylinders which were held together by a pair of long rods. The advantage of the Type H container was that it could be quickly broken down into its component parts and carried away from the landing site. Sample contents of each container are shown in Table E.

Organizing supply drops became the principal concern of most Resistance groups. Once radio contact had been established, a confirmation message would be broadcast by the BBC that a group could expect a delivery that evening. The process of delivery was always more or less the same and a typical *parachutage* is well described by shot-down Allied airman-turned-evader Thomas Teare:

As soon as darkness fell we would make our way to the prearranged dropping ground and then listen in silence for the sound of a lone aircraft; when we heard this we were to shine three red lights upwards, held in a straight line, at 100-metre intervals. I myself was to stand 100 metres from the end of the red line, and as the aircraft circled I was to flash the letter S with a white light... Each canister would bear the same number. If for example, we found they bore the mark 'No.15' we would know then that we must search for fifteen canisters. As each one was found it was to be carried to a hiding place in a nearby wood to await further transportation at a later date concealed in a load of hay.

As D-Day approached, and immediately afterwards, the number of supply drops increased significantly. André Hue, a Resistance figure who had gone to England and had enrolled in the SOE, was in charge of the *Hillbilly* network operating in Brittany. Parachuted into France with an advance party of French SAS troops, Hue was responsible for coordinating supply drops for the local maquis group. Each night he received a wealth of drops, including more SAS troops, PIAT anti-tank

weapons, mortars and even some jeeps, which required six parachutes each. But what was seemingly a success turned into a disaster. With so many planes flying overhead each night it was not long before the local German forces and the *Milice* figured out that there must be a sizeable Resistance group in the area – one too big to ignore. His forces coming under sustained German attack, Hue was forced to destroy most of the parachuted stores and disperse.

Nor were supply drops the answer to every maquis need. Agent Roger Millar and a local Resistance chief identified a problem and came up with a resourceful solution. Food was normally obtainable because the locals were generous and the Resistance usually had money that had been sent from England. However, Millar lists that they were short of things like 'boots, bicycles, tyres, petrol, blankets, socks, grease, biscuits and tinned food or chocolate for emergency rations.' Such things were available from the nearby German garrison. What the local maquis needed was a squad of men who specialized in organized theft. This in itself presented a problem. 'If we allowed them to become gangsters for one week they would never return to their regular work,' wrote Millar. 'It looked as though we must have another organization of gangsters, separate from our ordinary, "respectable" terrorists.'

Supply appears to have been a particular problem for the FTP, who complained they were kept out of the supply chain. Charles Tillon complained that of the hundreds of drops organized by the BCRA, only six were officially earmarked for FTP groups. They were also aware that ORA had arms stashed away – but these were jealously guarded. Instead the FTP advised its members to procure arms by other means. This included manufacturing weapons (incendiary bottles,

Waste not, want not: equipment salvaged after an FTP attack on a German column north of Kerien, in Brittany. (IWM MH11236)

bombs, grenades and tyre-bursters) or stealing industrial explosives from mines and enemy depots. They were greatly assisted by the chemist France Bloch-Serazin, who set up a laboratory in her Paris apartment to make detonators, explosives and cyanide capsules for the FTP. Before her arrest in 1942, she also went on missions to assess the quality of her products. One of the more enterprising means of obtaining arms was demonstrated by three FTP men in Dieppe, who surprised two German soldiers and threw them into the sea after taking their pistols.

TRAINING

In the early days, training in the *Combat* organization was supervised by Jacques Renouvin, whom Frenay described as an 'experienced brawler'. After November 1941 Renouvin formed a network of *Groupes Francs* dedicated to immediate action and to punishing collaborators. Reporting to Frenay on the state of readiness of his groups, Renouvin explained how every candidate for the rank of *Groupes Francs* chief hand-picked three or four promising recruits. Renouvin would get them together and put them through a 'boot camp' and teach them some theory. They would then select a target, make a reconnaissance, place some charges and then return the next day to survey the results before writing a report.

The next step in the training was to target collaborators and their interests in one of the larger cities, like Marseilles or Lyons. On the first mission Renouvin would tag along to bolster the group's confidence, but on the second mission he would leave the trainee chief in command. After the mission everyone would split up and then meet up the next day to discuss how the operation went. Renouvin was hard on his recruits and told Frenay: 'Not everybody I come across is that good. I've had to train a lot of my own people, but I guarantee you that by now they're real crack troops… If I spot any sissies, I get rid of them.'

The FTP supplemented their training with a considerable number of written manuals. The first manual to appear was a brochure entitled *Manuel du Légionnaire* (Legionary Manual), which at first glance ironically passed itself off as a publication for French fascists going to fight in Russia. Another brochure explained how to use explosives and the best way of destroying railway tracks, turntables, pylons, cables and so on. Other brochures covered topics as diverse as scouting, topography and group combat methods. One was entitled *How to Fight* and advised FTP members to put feelers out to the local community and to use them as their eyes and ears. Perhaps most usefully, the FTP produced a manual showing the operation of all small arms employed by the French, British, American and German armies.

The FTP also established a training regime for its officers. The courses for this school were written by Professeur Marcel Prenant, the FTP chief-of-staff and author of many FTP training guides, including the *Manuel du Légionnaire*. In total there were eight courses:

Course 1: guerrilla warfare
Course 2: group security in base and on the march
Course 3: action against enemy stores
Course 4: action against locales occupied by the enemy
Course 5: attacking enemy troops and convoys
Course 6: group defensive combat
Course 7: offensive combat against effective resistance
Course 8: concepts of topography, etc.

A liaison officer at work studying a map. Note his Colt pistol, compass, 'FS' knife and US M1 Carbine. The object by his right forearm is a radio set.
(IWM HU56019)

Towards the end of 1942 the FTP's supreme body, the CMN, issued advice to local commanders on how to conduct themselves in the run-up to an operation. It told them to prepare thoroughly and always to look to minimize damage to their men. More importantly, the note advised: 'Speak to your men; show them the importance of their mission, the grandeur of the cause they serve, raise their political comprehension and their morale, create between them a spirit of solidarity...'

Working with an FTP group, Jedburgh team member Thomas Macpherson saw this leadership style in action:

The leader of the FTP in the Department of Lot was a very strong character who went under the name of Commissar Georges. He actually held indoctrination classes as well as his military operations and exercised a degree of almost forced recruitment among the young people of the area, threatening their families. But once he got them on board, he did operate against the Germans.

As a rule, the scope of training was limited by the knowledge of the instructor, the availability of weapons and ammunition and the need for secrecy. Live-firing practise was rare – although when it did take place, supply containers were often used as targets because they were about the same size as a man.

Much of the training given to the Resistance in the run-up to D-Day came from SOE agents who had been rigorously trained in Britain. Without this training the Resistance would have had little idea as to how to safely use the equipment parachuted to them. SOE agent Roger Millar once went to a cellar where explosives were being prepared and recorded his verdict of the untutored bomb makers he found there:

> If the instructors from the training schools in England could have seen those Frenchmen making up charges the cellar would have looked to them like Dante's Inferno. Every conceivable school 'don't' was being done.

RESISTANCE TACTICS

While the bulk of the AS was in hiding waiting for D-Day, its direct-action groups were very much at work. In the early days, much of their effort was directed at punishing collaborators. Lists of the collaborators' names were published and there was talk of one group branding the more notorious collaborators with a swastika insignia. Approaching D-Day the direct action came in two distinct categories:

a) Slowing or stopping production of industry destined for German use and the sabotage of transport and lines of communication (rail, canals, roads, electric lines)
b) Attacking the forces of occupation, the Gestapo and their agents

To provide intelligence on industrial targets, a technical commission was formed of technicians from the different branches of industry. They made enquiries on the work being carried out for the enemy, defined the objectives that would cause the maximum disruption and suggested the most appropriate means of attack.

From the French point of view sabotage on the ground was infinitely preferable to Allied air raids. In their opinion the Allied bomber offensive caused unwanted civilian casualties for little productive effect. Resistance leaders argued that a single factory worker could cause far more damage than a squadron of bombers. Although the Nazis would take reprisals against the civilian population, horrible as it may seem, these reprisals were perhaps less hazardous to the majority than Allied bombing. FTP chief Charles Tillon gave some statistics on this. He recorded that from June to December 1941 the RAF carried out 60 bombing raids and 65 strafing attacks, during which many civilians died. During the same period, his groups carried out 107 acts of sabotage, set off 41 bombs and caused eight derailments. In 1942 there were 278 acts of sabotage compared to 168 Allied bombings.

A member of the Resistance sets an explosive charge on a railway line. Saboteurs would often use grenades as anti-tamper devices when planting explosives on a track. The grenade would be strapped to the underside of the rail and the pin removed. If anyone tried to remove the assembly, the grenade would fall free and detonate.
(IWM HU56936)

A prize target. Wrecked locomotives in an engine shed at the Annemasse railway depot after being sabotaged by the Resistance. (IWM ZZZ11837E)

Another good example of sabotage as the most effective form of attack came in July 1943. The RAF bombed the Peugeot works at Sochaux, which made tank turrets and aircraft engine parts for the Germans. The RAF missed the works and killed hundreds of civilians in the process. To avoid a repeat of this, the SOE organizer for the Jura region, Henri Rée, contacted Rudolphe Peugeot. Rée offered to keep the RAF away if the Peugeot family sabotaged their own factory. As proof of his credentials, Rée had the BBC broadcast an agreed message to demonstrate that he had the means of communicating with London. Hearing the broadcast, Peugeot gave Rée the plans to the plant allowing him to select where to place the explosives for the maximum effect. The Peugeot plant never fully recovered from the attack. Interestingly, when the Michelin family were approached with a similar proposal, they refused. The RAF was duly called in and flattened their tyre factory at Clermont-Ferrand.

Another top industrial target in France was the Schneider-Creusot arms producer near Lyons. In 1942 the RAF had unsuccessfully bombed the target and killed 1,000 French civilians in the process. Rather than risk repeating their failure, two French agents were parachuted in. Raymond Basset (codename *Mary*) and André Jarrot (*Goujean*) organized local sabotage teams and attacked the power stations supplying the plant. Through selective attacks by the Resistance on the power grid, production at Schneider-Creusot was crippled.

Sabotage was not limited to the use of explosives. Resistance leader Henri Frenay had Henri Garnier, an engineer in Toulouse, tamper with plans and blueprints for weapons and equipment. By altering the tolerances or making small millimetre deviations, the lifespan of guns and engines could be considerably reduced. Better still, the sabotage was almost impossible to detect. Both the SOE and OSS encouraged workers to perform simple acts of sabotage. The word sabotage derives from the French word for a wooden clog. In the same way that peasant workers might drop a clog into an Industrial Revolution-era machine, wartime French workers could toss a handful of sand or pebbles into a machine, with devastating results. They could re-route cargo shipments on the rail network, or leave a screw half undone. Better still, the SOE supplied abrasive grease that would quickly foul up moving parts on a machine or vehicle. The key to sabotage was in its being untraceable.

Of course, the French Resistance is most famous for blowing up trains – and rightly so. The most effective sabotage campaign conducted by the Resistance was against the railway network. Attacks were made against German troop and supply trains, tracks were cut, bridges blown and locomotives damaged. Between June 1943 and May 1944 a total of 1,822 locomotives were damaged, 200 passenger cars destroyed, 1,500 cars damaged, 2,500 freight cars destroyed and 8,000 damaged by Resistance action. In the first three months of 1944, the Resistance sabotaged 808 locomotives, compared to 387 damaged by air attack. However, when the weather began to clear and air attacks were stepped up, there were 292 sabotages against 1,437 locomotives hit by air strikes. These statistics do not tell the whole story, as they do not include the number of attacks that were foiled. The Resistance was so active that the Germans were forced to bring in reliable railway workers from Germany and put soldiers on trains.

When carrying out sabotage, care had to be taken not to harm French civilians. A wire strung across a road to decapitate a German motorcyclist would do the same to a passing civilian. In the same way, attacks on the railways had to be planned to avoid passenger trains. This is where the complicity of the *Cheminots* was vital. Roger Millar helped out on a rail mission with an FTP maquis group from Clairvaux. Arriving at the station signal box, the FTP leader introduced himself to the signalman with the words: 'We've come to blow up your box.' To which the signalman replied that a passenger service was still expected. The maquis leader said they would wait for it to go past before setting off the charges. The signalman agreed and asked to be tied up and locked in the station master's office to cover up his complicity.

Millar helped lay the charges. He says that he set three charges and linked them with detonating cord. At training school he had been taught to double-up the fuses, but had found that in the field this was impossible because of a lack of material. More charges were set 'in the hearts of the points' – the steel casings of these targets were very hard for the Germans to replace as hundreds of thousands had already been destroyed by Allied bombing. While Millar took care of this a maquisard placed charges round the telegraph poles. These charges looked like oversized pearl necklaces and were made from moulding lumps of plastic explosive around some detonator cord. When the passenger train had passed, Millar placed the detonators into the charges. They were preset to different times. All the agent had to do was select the required time, crush one end of the fuse to make it work – and not make a mistake. As Millar knew: 'a mistake might mean instant disintegration.'

Railway engine derailed following sabotage on the Grenoble–Marseilles line. (IWM MH11123)

A bridge destroyed over
the River Guil at Embrun.
(IWM HU57103)

Missions for D-Day

Until the end of May 1944, the Allies accepted that the best use for the Resistance was for it to lie low until specifically ordered into action – thus they would not rise up before Allied units could effectively support them. This policy was known as 'Block Planning' – calling the Resistance out to fight one region at a time. But would the French be disciplined enough to wait? Would news of the invasion be met with a national uprising? Almost at the last minute, and without de Gaulle's knowledge, SHAEF changed its policy on using the Resistance. Instead of piecemeal activation, the Resistance would be activated across the whole of France simultaneously. Although this meant that many Resistance groups would not receive any support from Allied troops and would almost certainly be attacked by Germans, Eisenhower wanted every bit of help when he most needed it – at the time of the landing when the Allies were trying to secure their beachheads in Normandy. To Eisenhower the success of the invasion was by no means a foregone conclusion.

Since the date of the invasion could not be given to the Resistance in advance, organizers were instructed to listen to BBC broadcasts on the 1st, 2nd, 15th and 16th of each month. If the invasion was imminent, they would hear the message 'l'heure des combats viendra' (the hour battle will come), which signified there would be a landing within 15 days. This message was broadcast on 1 June. The next day came a message comprising a line from a poem by Verlaine: 'Les sanglots longs de l'automne...' (the long sobs of autumn...), signalling that the landings were imminent. The reading of the second line of this verse would indicate that the invasion was set for the following day.

On 5 June, at 9.15pm the Resistance received the second line: '... *bercent mon cœur d'une langueur monotone*' (...wound my heart with a monotonous languor).

A series of plans had been developed with the assistance of the Resistance. When the time came, the BBC would broadcast the activation messages for these missions, which included:

Plan Vert (Green): destruction of the railways
Plan Rouge (Red): destruction of enemy ammunition dumps
Plan Bleu (Blue): destruction of power lines
Plan Violet (Purple): destruction of postal and telecommunications lines
Plan Jaune (Yellow): destruction of enemy command posts
Plan Noir (Black): destruction of enemy fuel depots
Plan Tortue (Tortoise): neutralization of the roads

On 5 June the Resistance in Normandy was told to enact *Plan Violet*. Perhaps one of the most important resistance efforts was to destroy German telephone wires and telecommunication cables. The French post and telegraph service, the PTT, provided London with details of underground telephone and telegraph lines used by the Germans. The Berlin–Paris cable was cut numerous times, making communication between Hitler's high command and the generals in Normandy so difficult they were forced onto the radio. Once the signals were broadcast by radio, they could be intercepted and were sent to Bletchley Park for

An eager group of maquisards study a map before an operation. Notice the commander's brassard with a Cross of Lorraine insignia. (IWM MH11125)

decryption. In the battle for Normandy this would give the Allies a vital advantage when the debates between Hitler and General von Kluge were being read daily by Churchill and Eisenhower. For example, on 5 August von Kluge told Hitler that a planned German counterattack would be a disaster. Pre-warned, the Allies were able to spring a trap, which netted and destroyed large German forces in the Falaise Gap.

The most famous of the missions was *Plan Vert* – the order to cut the critical military railroads. In May the SOE reported that 571 rail targets had been identified, the destruction of which would support the landings. In addition, Resistance leaders planned to disorganize the railways further with the planned non-cooperation of the rail trade unionists and management. It was estimated that rail traffic could be seriously hampered for eight to ten days after the Allied landings. In fact, during June a total of 486 rail cuts were reported. On 7 June 26 trunk lines were unusable, including the main lines between Avranches and St Lô, between St Lô and Cherbourg, and between St Lô and Caen. Until the end of June no trains crossed the area of Burgundy, through which ran all the main and secondary lines between the Rhône Valley and the Rhine. Virtually every train from Marseilles to Lyons was attacked, while rail lines north of Lille were cut.

Plan Vert was complemented by the plan to interfere with road traffic (*Plan Tortue*). To be effective, road sabotage required heavy equipment that could not be delivered to the Resistance in time. Therefore *Plan Tortue* focused on blocking roads through guerrilla actions. These operations were arguably the most common type of action undertaken by the Resistance, and they were backed not just by SOE agents, but by a significant number of SAS detachments, OSS 'Operational Groups' and the Jedburgh teams. These regular troops gave the Resistance a boost in terms of firepower, professional training and, albeit tactfully given, leadership. The SAS had machine-gun-armed jeeps parachuted to them, which allowed them to roam around in search of German convoys they could attack. One SAS group even had a 6-lb field gun dropped to them, much to the surprise of one German armoured car; but this example was a rarity.

Roads were blocked by fallen trees and trucks were attacked when they were forced to stop. Snipers would kill a German driver then vanish without trace. Thomas Macpherson took part in the operations against the German *Das Reich* division, which famously took 18 days to travel from Toulouse to Normandy – a journey that had previously taken three days. Macpherson had a small force of maquisards, too small to inflict any real damage on the German column, but enough to delay it, which was the aim.

First, the Resistance fighters blew a tree down across the road. The Germans tried to move it with an armoured car, but were forced to bring up a bulldozer tank from the rear to barge the trunk out of the way. After a long delay the tree was

cleared, whereupon a maquisard whom Macpherson had left behind opened fire with his Sten. This sent the German troops scattering and caused more delays and confusion. At the next roadblock, Macpherson bought down another tree, but this time hid two anti-tank mines underneath the trunk:

> The tank came along and this time they paused because they realized there might be a chap with a gun somewhere behind them. So they swept the area in around each side of the road for about a quarter of a mile behind. All this took a nice lot of time. Then they gave the all clear and the tank ploughed forward and there was a nice big bang. If you lose one track on a tank it slews round and blocks the road… It means a very long delay while they sent for another heavy vehicle.

At a third barricade several miles up the road, Macpherson blew two more trees down:

> This time in a crude and elementary way we booby-trapped it. Not on the ground, because I envisaged that they would see this, stop and send engineers up to see if there were mines on the ground, which there weren't. There was a lot of leaf above head height lying across the road and in those leaves, very precariously balanced, we left a couple of standard hand grenades with their pins out, so that the moment they were dislodged, the pins would fly off and in seven seconds the grenades would blow.

A liaison officer serving with the 3e Régiment Chasseurs Parachutistes (RCP) lands in Brittany on 24 June 1944. By sending uniformed soldiers in to help the Resistance the Allies hoped they would improve maquis moral. It was also hoped the uniform would give them some protection if caught. Although Hitler had issued orders to shoot all enemy servicemen operating behind German lines, whether in uniform or not, it was believed the Wehrmacht would adopt a more pragmatic approach. If they began shooting prisoners in uniform, perhaps the Allies would start doing the same. (IWM MH30648)

A member of the FFI uses a truck for cover during gun battles with German snipers in Dreux. (IWM EA33757)

In a separate incident Macpherson and a team of 27 FTP maquisards attempted to hold up a German armoured column by destroying a bridge. Two of the FTP men were ordered to wrap wet cloths around the barrels of their Sten guns. This had the effect of making the Stens sound like heavy machine guns to the Germans. When the leading halftrack of the German column reached the bridge, one of the maquisards detonated the explosives and set the vehicle on fire. A Panther tank approached the bridge, where another maquisard had been left in hiding. When the German tank reached the bridge, the hidden man threw a 'Gammon' grenade (see Plate E) at the tank and blew a track off. The road was blocked. As the remaining German tanks began shelling Macpherson's position and infantry began closing in, he ordered his maquisards to retreat to a waiting truck.

These continuous pinpricks caused enormous, potentially fatal delays. When *Das Reich* did finally arrive in the battle zone, it did so not as a collected unit, but in dribs and drabs. Another German division coming from Russia took a week to reach France, but then three weeks to cross from the French border to Caen in Normandy. The delays caused by the Resistance were of particular importance during the three-day storm that slowed down the Allied build up in Normandy and presented the Germans with a chance to move their reserves while the Allied air force was grounded by bad weather. One Allied assessment reported that the Germans were moving at just 25 per cent of their normal daily rate because of the constant attacks.

Perhaps the greatest failure of Resistance tactics occurred when it stopped acting like a guerrilla force and tried to take on the Germans in a pitched battle. As the French were kept in the dark over the Allied invasion plans, they had developed a strategy of their own. This was a scheme for the Resistance to seize large areas in the heart of France which would provide a landing area for supplies and an Allied airborne force, codenamed 'Force C'. Once established, Allied and French troops would then be able to attack the Germans from the rear. Although this plan was allowed to gain some ground, it was ultimately rejected by SHAEF. Further investigation of the landing sites revealed that they were only controlled by the Resistance as long as the Germans chose not to challenge them. Like all guerrilla forces, the maquis would not be able to resist the challenge of a regular army in a pitched battle and so, with all eyes on the landing beaches in Normandy, the plan was thought to be a distraction.

Although SHAEF rejected the plan, this did not filter down to the Resistance groups on the ground who still expected the arrival of Force C.

Three pitched battles ensued, on the Glières plateau, at Mont-Mouchet and perhaps most famously on the Vercors plateau. Although the Allies did begin supplying these Resistance 'redoubts', once the Germans realized how heavily concentrated the maquis were becoming, they could no longer ignore what was going on. Heavy assaults were mounted and although the resisters proved themselves to be tenacious fighters, they were either forced to retreat or defeated. In each case the failure of the Allies to supply mortars to combat the German mortars was one of the decisive factors against the resisters. The Resistance's casualties at Vercors were particularly heavy after the Germans used glider troops to negate the difficult ground.

A similar situation was encountered by André Hue in Brittany, the scene of some of the heaviest maquis action in the war. Several thousand maquisards had gathered near Saint Marcel – too many for the Germans to ignore. Although the maquis had received equipment drops and were supported by French SAS troops, they could offer only limited resistance when attacked. Hue described an unexpected problem during the battle, one against which the maquis was powerless:

> Now every weapon that the enemy possessed was brought to bear on our front line in a cacophony of shots and explosions which could not drown an even more sinister noise: the occasional crack of a single bullet. A man within feet of me slumped to the ground with blood spurting two feet into the air from the side of his neck… We had anticipated an infantry assault – possibly backed up with light armour – but snipers, a threat we had not met before, were difficult to counter. Within minutes of the first casualty another seven of our men lay dying within the farm complex: all had been shot from long range.

With the continued threat of snipers, the Saint Marcel maquis heard reports that the Germans were bringing up heavy armour. The maquisards were getting tired and, as the Germans had begun to gain ground, they were becoming discouraged. This was the time to give the order to disperse into the woods and to live to fight another day. Hue gave a final appreciation of the efforts of the maquis in battle:

> The majority of the younger men had never been in battle, and seeing their friends' brains and guts oozing on to the grass and mud made them sick in head and stomach. Just as terrifying to the young Frenchmen was the sight of those who were wounded and who yet had to lie without help. I was not surprised that so many had had enough. I was perhaps astonished that the number of defectors was so low.

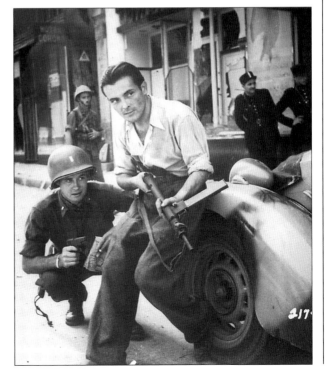

Reprisals

One cannot mention Resistance action in 1944 without detailing some of the reprisals taken by the Nazis on the civilian population. We have seen how, since 1941, the Germans had already begun shooting hostages in retaliation for Resistance attacks and how captured Resistance members could expect little mercy if captured. After the Allied invasion of Normandy, the forces of occupation – including the French *Milice* – increased the scope of their reprisals and committed some truly horrible atrocities in the process.

Following the Vercors uprising, there were huge reprisals against villages in the area, which included numerous incidents of rape, looting, the murder of civilians, the execution of wounded resisters and the mutilation of corpses. On 9 June, in response to Resistance action against elements of the *Das Reich* division in the town of Tulle, the Nazis took their revenge against the town population in lieu of there being any captured resisters. At random, the Germans hanged 99 people from the lampposts and balconies along the main street.

This same division was responsible for what has been described as the 'crowning event' of German atrocities in France. On 10 June, the day after Tulle, members of the SS *Der Führer* regiment entered the town of Oradour-sur-Glane. The population was ordered to assemble in the town square and a search was made of the buildings. Once assembled, all the men were taken away and split into groups, which were directed into barns and other buildings. Meanwhile the women and children were ordered inside the local church. The men were then machine

On 25 May 1944, these maquisards of the Maquis de Lantilly (Cote d'Or) have been captured and await execution, something a few of the Nazi soldiers appear to find amusing. (IWM MH11181)

gunned. Straw and bundles of wood were placed over the bodies and set alight – grenades were also thrown into the buildings. German soldiers then entered the church and placed an incendiary device on the communion table. The atmosphere inside the church quickly became asphyxiating, so the people inside broke open the church door to let in air. At this point the Germans began firing through the door and windows. In total, there were 642 victims, including 246 women and 207 children.

Although perhaps not on the same scale as Oradour-sur-Glane and Tulle, there were massacres all over France. Unable to get to grips with the elusive resisters, the Germans vented their rage and frustration on anyone they suspected was connected to the Resistance or had aided it. The following extract from the Nuremberg trials, focusing on German war crimes in the region of Nice in July 1944, perhaps illustrates the savagery innocent people faced in the last days of occupation:

> Having been attacked … by several groups of Maquis in the region, by way of reprisals, a Mongolian detachment, still under the SS, went to a farm where two French members of the Resistance had been hidden. Being unable to take them prisoner, these soldiers then took the proprietors of that farm, (the husband and wife), and after subjecting them to numerous atrocities (knifing, rape, et cetera) they shot them down with sub-machine guns. Then they took the son of these victims who was only three years of age, and, after having frightfully tortured him, they crucified him on the gate of the farmhouse.

Parisians building barricades in the Paris uprising of August 1944. More than 600 barricades were set up around the city, preventing the Germans from making an effective defence. (IWM MH11152)

Paris sees the Germans go. Nazi POWs after the liberation of Paris on 25 August 1944. (NARA 196288)

A FINAL RECKONING

The humiliation of 1940 gave way to the recriminations of Liberation. It is believed that 100,000 Resistance members had been killed during their four-year struggle for liberation. With understandable fury, yesterday's oppressed turned on known collaborators. Those girls that had gone with Germans were dragged through the streets and had their heads shaved; many others were shot in a wave of terror. With the Germans gone, the old guard of the Resistance shook their heads at the number of closet resisters that had sprung out of the woodwork in the last days of the struggle. They even had a name for these Johnny-come-latelies: the FFS – *Forces Françaises de Septembre* – or *Septemberists* for short. Others waited on tenterhooks for the communists to reveal their hand: would there be civil war or would the FTP hand in their guns? Thankfully they chose to go the way of the ballot box.

Sadly, the SOE's F Section personnel were cold-shouldered and ordered out of France. A typical case was Roger Landes, who, although British, had been raised in France. He became the chief Resistance leader in Bordeaux after the regional leader and OCM member André Grandclément was exposed as a Gestapo informer. After Bordeaux was liberated, de Gaulle visited and told Landes, who was proudly wearing a British uniform, to get out of the city within two hours. The story was the same all over France. Following the collapse of 1940, de Gaulle was hell bent on claiming the liberation of 1944 as a French victory. His motives are understandable, but it must have left a bitter taste in the mouths of many who fought alongside the Resistance.

Once Hitler was dead and peace had returned to Europe, the countless numbers of deportees and prisoners of war began returning to France. Displaced people and refugees were on the move and life slowly but surely began to return to normal amid the ruins. Had the Resistance been worth it? In the eyes of the initially sceptical Allied personnel, the answer was a resounding 'yes'. If nothing else, the bravery and self-sacrifice of the Resistance helped save the lives of many Allied soldiers. As one of the Normandy invasion planners, Ralph Ingersoll, recorded in his book *Top Secret*:

> … what cut the ice with us was the fact that when we came to France the resistance was so effective that it took half a dozen real live German divisions to contend with it, divisions which might otherwise have been on our backs in the Bocage. And it made the most cynical sit up and take notice when we learned from German field officers that the Germans in central

After the Liberation a French girl has her head shaved as punishment for sleeping with a German. (ARC 531211)

France were truly terrified, had to live under arms, could not move freely, had lost all control in sizable sectors even before we came… It was a military fact that the French were worth at least a score of divisions to us, maybe more.

Members of the 'Maquis Louis' pose for a team photo with SOE officers. Note the men with scarves made from parachutes. (IWM HU68064)

Members of the FFI carry out the death sentence of six people convicted of collaborating with the Germans in Grenoble. It is uncertain how many were executed in the purge that followed Liberation, with estimates varying from 10,000 to 100,000 victims. (NARA 196291)

BIBLIOGRAPHY & FURTHER READING

There follows a list of some of the most useful books consulted here. Among them the memoirs of Frenay and Tillon are highly recommended, along with the indispensable studies of M. R. D. Foot, Henri Michel and Pierre Lorain. For an in-depth study, the works of Henri Amoroux are also recommended, covering almost every aspect of French life and Resistance during the Nazi occupation.

Astier, Emmanuel d' (trans. Humphrey Hare), *Seven Times Seven Days*, Macgibbon & Kee, London (1958)

Bénouville, Guillain de, *Le Sacrifice du Matin*, Robert Laffont, Paris (1946)

Braddon, Russell, *Nancy Wake: the story of a very brave woman*, Cassell, London (1956)

Buckmaster, Maurice J., *Specially Employed: the story of British Aid to French patriots of the Resistance*, London, Batchworth Press (1952)

Casey, William, *The Secret War Against Hitler*, Simon & Schuster, London (1989)

Foot, M. R. D., *SOE in France*, HMSO, London (1966)

– *Resistance: an analysis of European resistance to Nazism, 1940–1945*, Eyre Methuen, London (1976)

– *Six Faces of Courage*, Eyre Methuen, London (1978)

Frenay, Henri, *The Night will End*, Coronet Books, London (1976)

Harrison, Gordon A., *Cross-Channel Attack*, United States Army, Washington DC (1951)

Hastings, Max, *Das Reich: resistance and the march of the 2nd SS Panzer Division through France, June 1944*, Joseph, London (1981)

Hue, André & Ewen Southby-Tailyour, *The Next Moon*, Viking, London (2004)

Ingersoll, Ralph, *Top Secret*, Harcourt, Brace & Co., New York (1946)

Lorain, Pierre, *Secret Warfare: the arms and techniques of the Resistance*, Orbis Publishing, London (1983)

Michel, Henri (trans. Douglas Parmée), *The Second World War*, Deutsch, London (1975)

– (trans. Richard Barry), *The Shadow War: resistance in Europe, 1939–1945*, Deutsch, London (1972)

Millar, George, *Maquis*, William Heinemann, London (1945)

Passy, Colonel (pseud. André Dewavrin), *Souvenirs*, 3 vols, R. Solar, Monte Carlo (1947–51)

Paxton, Robert, *Vichy France: Old Guard and New Order, 1940–1944*, Knopf, New York (1972)

Rémy, *L'opération Jericho*, Editions de Crémille, Genève (1972)

Schoenbrun, David, *Soldiers of the Night: the story of the French Resistance*, Robert Hale, London (1980)

Seaman, Mark, *Bravest of the Brave: the true story of Wing Commander Tommy Yeo-Thomas, SOE secret agent, codename 'the White Rabbit'*, Michael O'Mara, London (1997)

Stafford, David, *Secret Agent: the true story of the Special Operations Executive*, BBC, London (2000)

Teare, T. D. G., *Evader*, Hodder & Stoughton, London (1954)

Tillon, Charles, *Les F.T.P. Témoignage pour servir à l'histoire de la Résistance*, Juillard, Paris (1962)

Wellsted, Ian, *SAS: With the Maquis – In Action with the French Resistance, June–September 1944*, Greenhill Books, London (1994)

Also recommended are several films: Jean-Pierre Melville's 1969 *L'Armée des Ombres* (Army in the Shadows) is widely recognized as a Resistance classic and was re-released in 2006; Marcel Ophuls' *Le chagrin et la pitié* (The Sorrow and the Pity; 1969), a documentary on Clermont-Ferrand during the occupation, which interviews resisters and collaborators alike. For a sobering, but mercifully short French perspective on *Nacht und Nebel* see Alain Resnais' 1955 *Nuit et Brouillard* (Night and Fog). There have been a number of useful English documentaries including the BBC's *Agent* and *Gladiators of World War II* series.

COLOUR PLATE COMMENTARY

A: MAQUISARD, 1944

A typical maquisard from the later period of occupation, armed with the Sten Mk II, which was dropped to the Resistance in enormous quantities. The Mk II was in many respects a crude weapon, but it was easily hidden, very easy to use and was designed to fire German 9mm Parabellum cartridges (1). The Mk II could also be manufactured with a suppressor for undercover operations (2). The suppressed version is shown with the 'skeleton' butt variation rather than the tubular one held by the figure – both were common. The Sten's magazine held 32 rounds, but because of the gun's tendency to jam, many users would only load 30 rounds into a magazine. In order to facilitate reloading empty magazines (3), Stens were delivered to the Resistance with a loader (4).

To fulfil the legal criteria that combatants must wear a distinguishing mark to be afforded the proper treatment if

wounded or captured, armbands were worn by members of the Resistance in action, three examples of which are shown here (5). The most typical devices used were the French tricolour and the Cross of Lorraine symbol. This cross was the symbol used by Joan of Arc (1412–31) in her struggle to liberate France from the forces of occupation, who were at that time – ironically enough – the English. Another almost mandatory item of uniform was the beret, which is of Basque origin. However, some photographs show resisters wearing a French army *Casque Adrian* (6), occasionally with the initials 'FFI' painted on the front. The first decoration is the *Ordre de la Libération* (7), which was created in November 1940 by General de Gaulle to reward those fighting for the liberation of France. The second decoration is the *Médaille de la Résistance* (8), which was created in 1943 and awarded to approximately 64,000 people – almost one third posthumously. Also shown are two ID cards of the period (9), ration coupons (10) – of which the British supplied forgeries – and a selection of underground newspapers (11), including *Combat* and *Libération*.

B: THE PASSAGE INTO SPAIN

Probably the first real organized Resistance action came with the creation of the evasion networks. Britain even formed MI9, a new branch of the secret service for making contact with and setting up the ways and means of getting service personnel out of occupied Europe. In addition to Allied servicemen, persecuted civilians and on-the-run resisters also looked to make contact with an escape circuit.

Although there was the possibility of taking a boat across the Channel, many individuals preferred the arduous journey over the Pyrenees into Spain and from there to British-held Gibraltar or neutral Portugal. Until the Germans occupied the southern zone this route was perhaps the most simple – after November 1942 it became much harder and evaders were sent to concentration camps if captured. Nor was it an easy matter to explain oneself to the Spanish authorities, who, although technically neutral, served a fascist government after all. Many evaders ended up stuck in a typhus-ridden internment camp waiting months to be tracked down by staff

A poster sporting a portrait of Marshal Pétain has been defaced by Resistance emblems. The 'V', standing variously for vengeance or victory, and the cross of Lorraine – the symbol of French heroine Joan of Arc – had been adopted by de Gaulle's Free French movement. Another popular piece of graffiti guaranteed to enrage the Germans was the initials 'RAF'. (IWM MH11122)

of the French consulate (who were informed by the Resistance of members on the run) before they were given permission to continue.

C: A LYSANDER PICKUP

Here an SOE agent is landed into France and a member of the Resistance is picked up. This fellow carries important documents which will be given to de Gaulle's BCRA intelligence service in London. For his troubles the pilot also collects some bottles of wine from his Resistance comrades.

The British Westland Lysander was initially used as a spotter plane, but was withdrawn from this role after suffering heavy loses in the Battle for France. Instead it became famous for Special Operations work, where it acquired the nickname the 'Spy Taxi'. Although the Lysander had found itself easy prey for the Luftwaffe, flying at night it was perfect for landing and taking off in small fields and had a range of up to 1,448km (900 miles) if equipped with a reserve tank. Originally designed to carry a pilot and one passenger, the Lysander was stripped of its weapons so it could, at a push, carry three passengers. A ladder was mounted on the left side of the fuselage to speed up the access and egress of passengers. From the beginning of 1942, the Lysanders were complemented by American Lockheed 'Hudson' light bombers, which could carry up to a dozen passengers.

D: GESTAPO ARREST, 1943

The sound every agent and resister dreaded was the screech of brakes followed by shouts in German. Caught moving between safe houses, carrying a wireless transmitter in a suitcase, this radio operator has been tracked by the Germans for several weeks. Carelessly the radio man continued to broadcast from the same location and did not take the necessary precautions – like changing frequencies every 5–10 minutes. When the Germans were close to finding their man several Gestapo officers drove out in their favoured Traction-Avant Citroën automobiles looking for the suspect.

There were endless 'controls' where the Germans and the Vichy police would check papers and examine the contents of suitcases. These controls were particularly heavy at railway stations and required a certain ingenuity and enormous luck to overcome. Arriving at a train station with a radio set hidden in a case, one agent saw there was a control in operation. Seeing a young boy having difficulty with a large suitcase, the agent offered to swap bags with the lad. The agent confidently walked through the control with the boy's case and, on the other side of the control, swapped cases back over. The boy then told of his relief that the agent had not been stopped carrying the suitcase. When asked why, the boy revealed his suitcase was full of pistols.

E: RESISTANCE ARMS

The French Resistance was supplied with a variety of weapons and sabotage equipment of which, along with the Sten, the following were the most common. The .303 calibre British Bren gun (1) had been initially developed in Czechoslovakia (the designation BREN stands for BRno-ENfield) and was manufactured in the UK after 1937. It was, according to many sources, one of the best light machine guns of its time. One of the most sought-after weapons was the British Lee-Enfield rifle (2 – here the No.4 Mk I 1939 model), which was supplied in large numbers and included a

bayonet. After July 1944 the Americans began to supply the 1941 model Winchester semi-automatic carbine US M1 (3) and, as a replacement to the Sten, the US M3 (1943) submachine gun (4).

In terms of personal weapons, the Resistance was supplied with large numbers of pistols, including the Webley Mk IV Revolver (5), which was widely distributed but considered somewhat outmoded – resisters preferred the American Colt Automatic (model 1911-A1) (6). The Fairbairn-Sykes (FS) knife (7) was designed by two ex-Shanghai municipal policemen – William Fairbairn and Eric A. Sykes – who were SOE's 'silent killing' instructors. Fairbairn was a martial arts expert while Sykes excelled in pistol shooting. As can be imagined, hardened on the mean streets of pre-war Shanghai, their philosophy was very much kill-or-be-killed. Their fighting techniques were so effective and the candidates so honed, that at least one SOE agent feared he might accidentally kill someone by a reflex action.

Also shown are the two most common grenades supplied to the Resistance: the British Mills Grenade No. 36 Mk I (8) and the 'Gammon' grenade (9), which was actually a 1kg (0.45lb) lump of plastic explosive, covered in a cloth skirt with a detonator on top. When thrown the safety pin would

The Bren gun was a particular favourite of Resistance fighters, as shown by this smiling resister at Chateaudun. (IWM EA33756)

disengage and the charge would explode on contact with deadly effect.

F: ARMS AND CONTAINERS

The Type C container (1) was perfect for larger equipment like the American Model AT M-1 A-1 Bazooka (2) or the British PIAT anti-tank weapon (3). In the absence of artillery or mortars, both these weapons afforded the Resistance a considerable punch against enemy vehicles, installations and even trains. For smaller loads the container could be divided into three compartments by the insertion of wooden disks. The parachute (4) was housed in the top of the container and fixed in place by a strap on each side (5). The Type H Container (6) in fact comprised five drums that were held together by two metal rods. The container is 1.7m (5ft 7in.) long, including the parachute housing and the impact cone on the bottom, with a diameter of 0.35m (1ft 2in). The maximum internal space of the container was 1.3m (4ft 3in.). The smaller compartments were perfect for storing small arms and, in particular, sabotage equipment and grenades (7). The type H had a distinctive shock absorber at its base (8) which was formed by a hollow, conical crumple zone. For secret operations work, both types were painted black.

G: *PLAN TORTUE*

Plan Tortue was originally envisaged as a pre-D-Day means of making French roads impassable to German traffic, but due to a lack of specialist equipment for destroying the roads it became a series of guerrilla attacks. By denying the country routes and lanes to German forces, the Resistance forced the Germans onto main highways where they were more prone to Allied air attacks. Like all Resistance operations, to be successful their attacks had to be hit-and-run by nature.

Although the action against *Das Reich* is perhaps the best-known example, there were numerous attacks against German troop movements all over France. In the south, the celebrated Spanish maquis chief, Cristino García, pulled off many such operations, notably on 13 July 1944 when he and 19 Spanish guerrillas ambushed and shot up a German troop convoy of 60 trucks. At the 'battle of La Madeleine' on 25 August 1944 García attacked a column of 1,200–1,500 German troops and armoured vehicles with just 31 Spaniards and four Frenchmen. After Garcia's men blew a bridge in front of the Germans and mined the road behind the column, the Germans were boxed in by forest on either side of the road. García's small force moved along the column spraying it with fire, making the Germans think they faced a much larger force. Trapped on the road, the Germans began negotiating, but refused to surrender to 'terrorists'. A truce was declared and the Germans taken to the local Gendarmerie, whose authority they recognized. Meanwhile, fighting broke out on the column again but was suspended when García received a reinforcement of 70 FTP fighters. After a brief fight the Germans gave up. A total of 1,100 soldiers surrendered, while their commander shot himself in disgrace.

H: RESISTANCE AND THE SAS

A local maquis chief and several French SAS troops meet a column of American Sherman tanks in Brittany to direct them towards a dug-in German position. Maquis operations in Brittany were so effective that the region is credited with

This photograph shows a group of maquisards carrying bedrolls and equipment bags. The presence of what appear to be American forces in the centre of the picture suggests this photo was taken after Liberation and shows the maquis coming down from the hills with their possessions. (IWM MH28283)

liberating itself. For the Allied troops, having Resistance fighters available to guide and assist them was of immeasurable benefit. This is explained first hand by Ralf Ingersoll:

To an army on the advance, there is all the difference in the world being able to roll through a town after smashing a single road block and having to stop to hunt out the half a hundred enemy who can fight you house-to-house with automatic weapons, and who will swarm in on your supply trains if you by-pass them. From St Lô to the German border, we never had to worry about a town in our rear. Let one American vehicle appear even in a sizeable city and its inhabitants would have the German garrison dead or disarmed a few hours later. The Maquis' traps were all set and their jaws sprang fast and savagely. Every scout car making an advanced reconnaissance was not one pair of eyes but a score – 'There are Germans in that woods, perhaps a thousand of them, but they have no vehicles; over beyond that hill, around the turn there is a tank trap; but you have nothing to fear going down *that* road; Uncle Henry was there this morning and the Germans went last night.' The effect on the morale of an army advancing so, amongst friends, is a mighty imponderable.

INDEX

References to illustrations are shown in **bold**. Plates are shown with page and caption locators in brackets.